THE UNOFFICIAL
HOLY BIBLE
FOR
MINECRAFTERS
OLD TESTAMENT

Stories from the Bible Told Block by Block

❮ CHRISTOPHER MIKO AND GARRETT ROMINES ❯

SKY PONY PRESS
NEW YORK

Sky Pony Press books may be purchased in bulk at special discounts for sales promotion, corporate gifts, fund-raising, or educational purposes. Special editions can also be created to specifications. For details, contact the Special Sales Department, Sky Pony Press, 307 West 36th Street, 11th Floor, New York, NY 10018 or info@skyhorsepublishing.com.

Sky Pony® is a registered trademark of Skyhorse Publishing, Inc.®, a Delaware corporation.

Minecraft® is a registered trademark of Notch Development AB. The Minecraft game is copyright © Mojang AB.

Visit our website at www.skyhorsepublishing.com.

10 9 8 7 6 5 4 3 2 1

Library of Congress Cataloging-in-Publication Data is available on file.

Cover design by Brian Peterson
Cover photos by Christopher Miko

ISBN: 978-1-5107-0225-7
Ebook ISBN: 978-1-63450-844-5

Printed in China

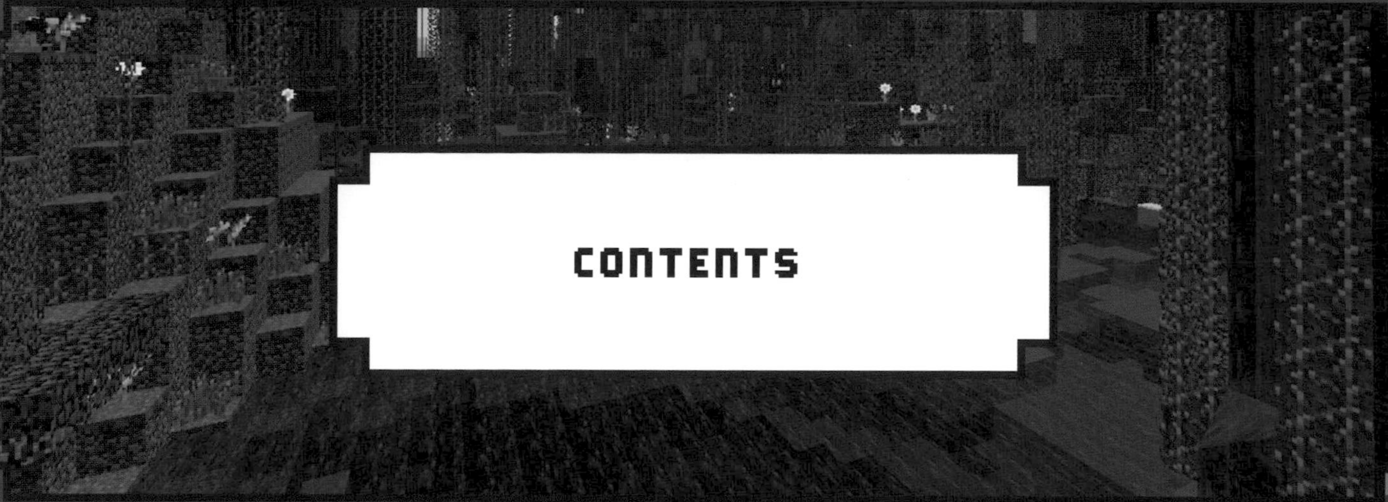

CONTENTS

DEDICATION

I WOULD LIKE TO DEDICATE THIS BOOK to my loving wife Lindsey. She endured me making it during the first year of our marriage. God bless her.

—Chris

I give glory to God in the highest praise for his blessings upon me, and to my friend and coauthor Chris Miko.

—Garrett

FOREWORD

WE ARE ALL GOD-SEEKING PEOPLE from the time we are born. The Bible is God's story about Himself and His relationship with human beings. Children who wish to learn more about the Bible and about God are blessed children! Bible stories inspire young people to grow in ways beyond their imagination. They will use these stories to become wonderful human beings.

As parents, it can be difficult to get children to read the Bible. In the *Unofficial Holy Bible for Minecrafters*, children will engage the Bible in a way that they enjoy. God's Creation story is full of profound life lessons. There are many answers in this book to challenges children may be facing in their own lives. Kids will learn from these stories how to be strong and courageous. Jesus faced bullies and had allies. He experienced peer-pressure and had to become comfortable with His identity as the Son of God. The Bible is an essential part of knowing and learning about our true selves. Scripture provides a blueprint and structure for how to live a wonderful life.

The colorful illustrations in this marvelous work bring biblical characters to life in a way far beyond what I could have ever imagined having available to me as a child. The illustrations were created in the video game, Minecraft, and provide a unique setting for the stories. This also further teaches parents to embrace the new world of youth and gaming and learn how it can be used as a resource in education overall.

I encourage the Christian community to share this book with their loved ones and to facilitate further discussion about God and the Bible in their homes and communities. This book definitely makes it more fun!

TERRY A. SMITH,
Lead Pastor, The Life Christian Church

LETTER TO PARENTS

DEAR PARENTS,

If your child is one of the mass millions who enjoys playing Minecraft, and you want to encourage your child to learn more and take a stronger interest in reading the Bible, *The Unofficial Holy Bible for Minecrafters* provides an excellent opportunity to introduce Bible stories in a fun and exciting way.

This beautifully illustrated book, full of over 250 amazing images, will enable the child not to just read the Bible stories, but to understand them in a way he or she can incorporate the messages into everyday decision-making.

With these stories, children will explore competency, autonomy, and self-identity from a new perspective. The Minecraft game gives players the opportunity to be creative, solve problems, and interact. In many ways, that is what we want our kids to do with the Bible stories. Bible stories serve to teach our children about how God interacts in the world and how He would want us to interact in the world.

The Unofficial Holy Bible for Minecrafters uses the world of Minecraft to capture the imagination of children and is cutting edge. It joins a long line of contemporary methods used to introduce the Bible to children.

Sincerely,
Rev. Dr. Wanda M. Lundry

THE CREATION STORY

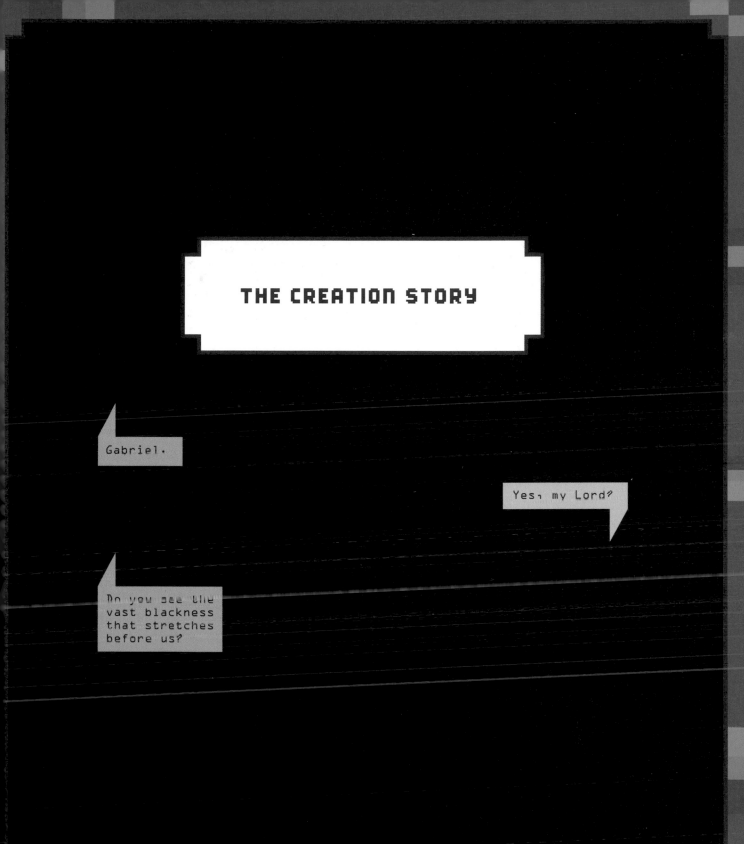

Gabriel.

Yes, my Lord?

Do you see the vast blackness that stretches before us?

We shall begin with a big bang!

IN THE BEGINNING, GOD CREATED THE HEAVENS AND EARTH.

THE EARTH WAS WITHOUT FORM AND SHAPE. DARKNESS WAS ON THE FACE OF THE DEEP.

GOD CALLED THE LIGHT "DAY," AND THE DARKNESS, "NIGHT," AND THE EVENING AND MORNING OF THE FIRST DAY PASSED.

Where should I begin
with this world? I think
I will start with water.

ON THE SECOND DAY, GOD BROUGHT
ALL WATERS TOGETHER UNDER
THE HEAVENS. EVENING CAME, AND
MORNING CAME, AND SO PASSED
THE SECOND DAY.

GOD THEN PUSHED THE WATERS BACK, SHOWING DRY LAND. HE CALLED THE DRY LAND "EARTH," AND THE WATER, "OCEANS." GOD THEN COMMANDED THE EARTH TO BE FRUITFUL, SO THE GRASS GREW, ALONG WITH THE FLOWERS, BUSHES, AND TREES. AND GOD SAW WHAT HE HAD CREATED AND CALLED IT GOOD. SO PASSED THE EVENING AND MORNING OF THE THIRD DAY ON EARTH.

I will create all living things that will spring up from this good Earth.

THEN GOD MADE THE SUN.

AND GOD FILLED THE HEAVENS WITH SHINING STARS.

AND HE MADE THE MOON. THE EVENING CAME AND SO DID MORNING ON THE FOURTH DAY.

GOD THEN CREATED ALL CREATURES THAT MOVED AND SWAM IN THE WATERS, AND EVERY KIND OF BIRD; AND GOD SAW THAT IT WAS GOOD. SO PASSED THE FIFTH DAY.

The Earth needs life, and by My Word, I shall give life to it.

GOD THEN MADE WILD ANIMALS, CATTLE, SHEEP, PIGS, AND ALL SORTS OF CREATURES TO LIVE ON THE EARTH. HE SAW WHAT HE HAD CREATED, AND IT WAS GOOD.

I will create you in My very own image. You will have free will to choose, and you will be My most precious creation.

AS HE WORKED ON THE SIXTH DAY, GOD DECIDED TO DO SOMETHING VERY SPECIAL. HE TOOK UP THE DUST FROM THE EARTH AND FORMED IT INTO A MAN. FROM THERE, HE BREATHED LIFE INTO HIM. MAN WAS CREATED TO WORSHIP AND LOVE HIM. GOD CALLED THIS FIRST MAN "ADAM" AND PLACED HIM IN THE GARDEN OF EDEN.

GOD SPOKE TO ADAM, GUIDING HIM IN THE WAYS OF THE LORD. FOR MANY DAYS AND NIGHTS, HE LIVED IN THE GARDEN. ADAM WAS HAPPY TO BE IN THE GARDEN, BUT HE FELT ALONE.

You may eat from every tree in the garden, but not from the tree in the center of the garden. That is the tree with the knowledge of good and evil. I say to you, My child, be warned, if you eat from the tree, you will surely die.

I shall obey.

GOD CALLED ON ADAM AND PUT HIM INTO A DEEP SLEEP. FROM ADAM, HE TOOK A RIB BONE AND CREATED A WOMAN.

Adam, it is not good that man should be alone. I will provide a partner for you. She will be the opposite of you, but like you, special in every way. She will complete you.

Oh Lord, she is perfect in every way! My heart is bursting with this feeling. I will call this feeling "Love." Eve, you are bone of my bone, flesh of my flesh, and we shall be happy forever.

I am Eve, and we shall be happy all the days of our lives.

GOD BROUGHT THE WOMAN TO ADAM. ADAM LOOKED UPON HER AND WAS VERY HAPPY.

ON THE SIXTH DAY, GOD COMPLETED ALL THE WORK AND SO HE STOPPED. HE TOLD ADAM AND EVE TO HAVE FUN, BUT REMINDED THEM NOT TO EAT FROM THE FORBIDDEN TREE. THEN HE WENT TO REST.

So, do you wanna build a house?

Nah, let's go swimming.

MAN'S LOSS OF PARADISE

Now can I cook, or can't I?

Yes, the Earth is truly beautiful to us angels.

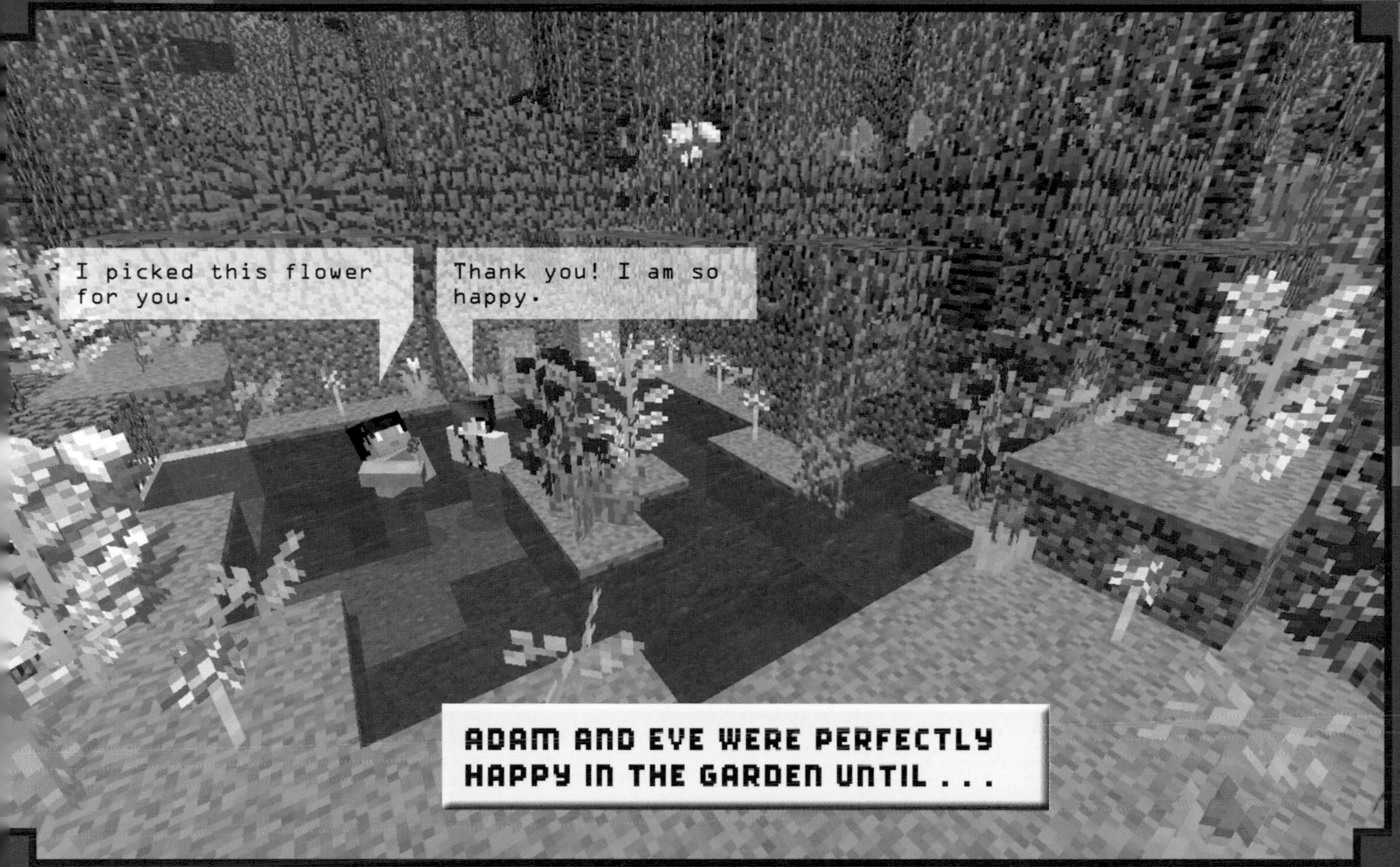
I picked this flower for you.
Thank you! I am so happy.
ADAM AND EVE WERE PERFECTLY HAPPY IN THE GARDEN UNTIL . . .

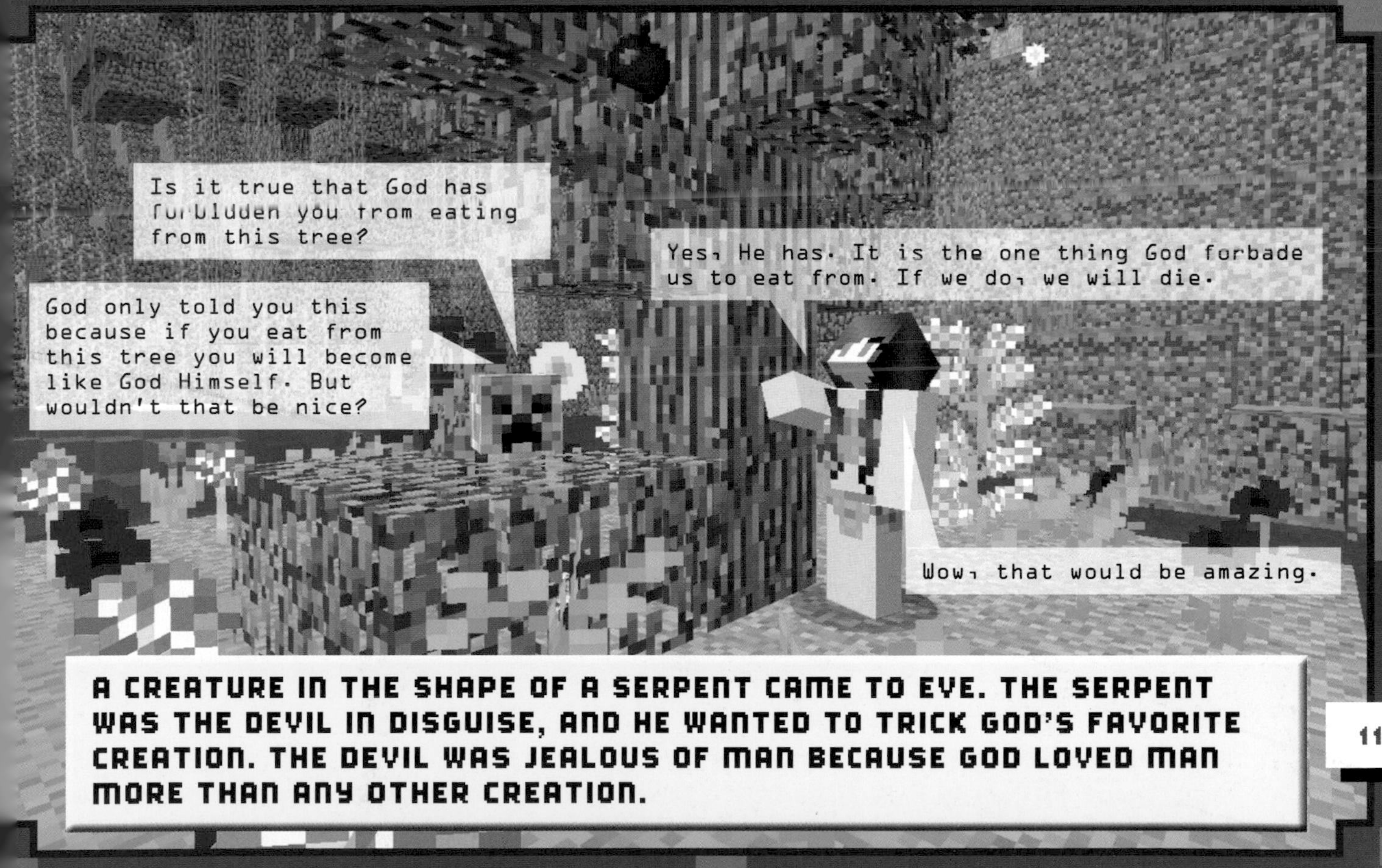
Is it true that God has forbidden you from eating from this tree?
Yes, He has. It is the one thing God forbade us to eat from. If we do, we will die.
God only told you this because if you eat from this tree you will become like God Himself. But wouldn't that be nice?
Wow, that would be amazing.
A CREATURE IN THE SHAPE OF A SERPENT CAME TO EVE. THE SERPENT WAS THE DEVIL IN DISGUISE, AND HE WANTED TO TRICK GOD'S FAVORITE CREATION. THE DEVIL WAS JEALOUS OF MAN BECAUSE GOD LOVED MAN MORE THAN ANY OTHER CREATION.

THE DEVIL WAS LYING TO EVE, BUT SHE DID NOT KNOW AND QUICKLY FORGOT THAT GOD'S RULES WERE THERE TO PROTECT HER. SHE TOOK THE FRUIT FROM THE TREE OF KNOWLEDGE AND ATE IT!

AS EVE TOOK A BITE, SHE FELT THE SURGE OF KNOWLEDGE CONSUME HER, AND THE FEELING WAS GREAT.

THE GOOD FEELING DIDN'T LAST LONG. ADAM AND EVE SUDDENLY KNEW THE BAD THINGS OF THE WORLD. THEY WERE AFRAID AND HID.

He is going to be so mad at us.

We are going to be in such big trouble!

What have you done, My child?

GOD, LOOKING DOWN ON THE EARTH, KNEW WHAT ADAM AND EVE HAD DONE, AND HE WAS SAD. HE WENT TO SPEAK WITH THEM.

She did it!

ADAM BLAMED EVE.

It tricked me.

EVE BLAMED THE SERPENT.

My children, I am sorry, but you must go. A time will come when I will redeem all men, and the sin will be washed away. But for now, paradise is lost.

Please, Lord, forgive us and let us stay.

ADAM AND EVE HAD TO LEAVE THE GARDEN, AND BECAUSE OF THEIR SIN, THEY AND ALL THEIR DESCENDANTS WERE NOW SEPARATED FROM GOD. BUT GOD HAD A PLAN TO BRING MAN BACK TO SALVATION.

CAIN AND ABEL

IN TIME, ADAM AND EVE SETTLED OUTSIDE OF EDEN. THEY HAD TWO SONS: CAIN AND ABEL.

ABEL'S JOB WAS TO CARE FOR THE FLOCKS.

AND CAIN TOOK CARE OF THE SOIL.

My sons, God commands us to give sacrifice to show our thanks in all He gives us.

I cannot wait to give thanks to God. I will give Him plenty!

The time has come for us to give our share.

I will give very little!

CAIN BROUGHT SOME LEFTOVERS FROM HIS HARVEST.

ABEL ALSO BROUGHT OFFERINGS, BUT HIS WAS THE BEST HE HAD TO OFFER.

THE LORD LOOKED WITH FAVOR UPON ABEL, BUT WAS NOT PLEASED WITH CAIN.

17

I hate my brother! God loves him more.

Why are you angry?

THEN THE LORD SPOKE TO CAIN.

Why should you love Abel more? Am I not the first born?

If you do what is right, you will be accepted. But if you do not do what is right, sin will take over your heart. There will be no end to the bad things you will do.

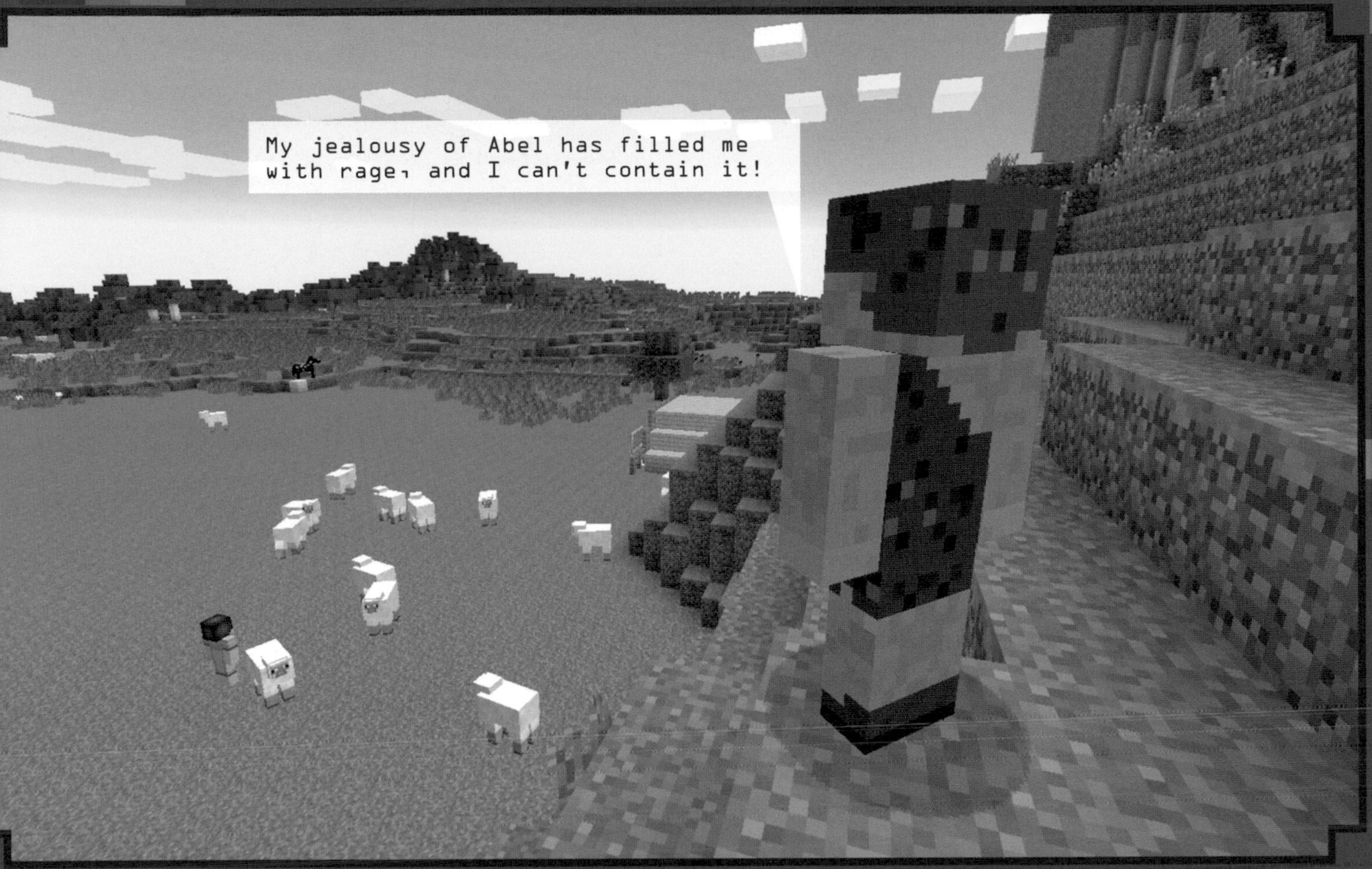
My jealousy of Abel has filled me
with rage, and I can't contain it!

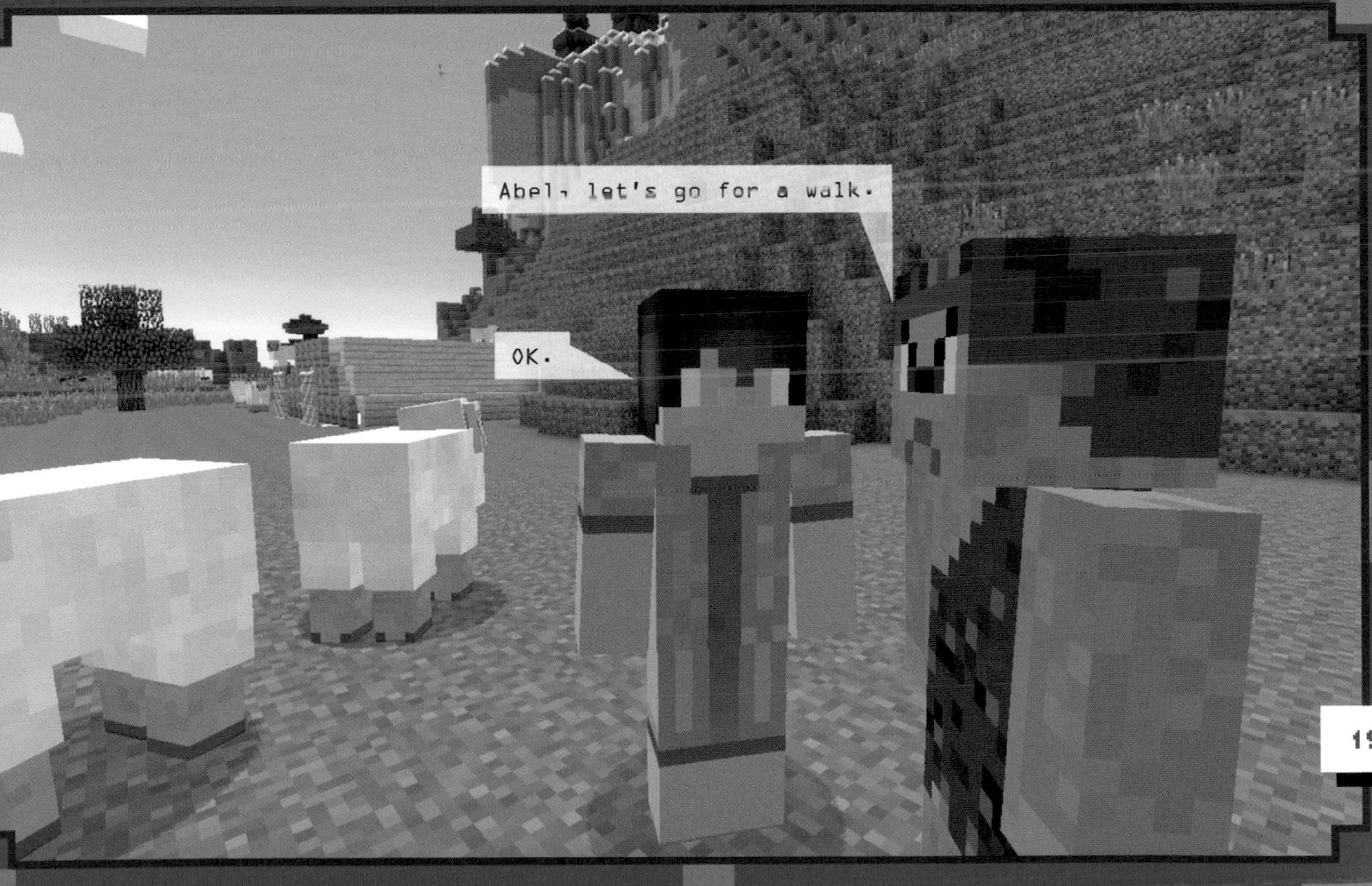
Abel, let's go for a walk.
OK.

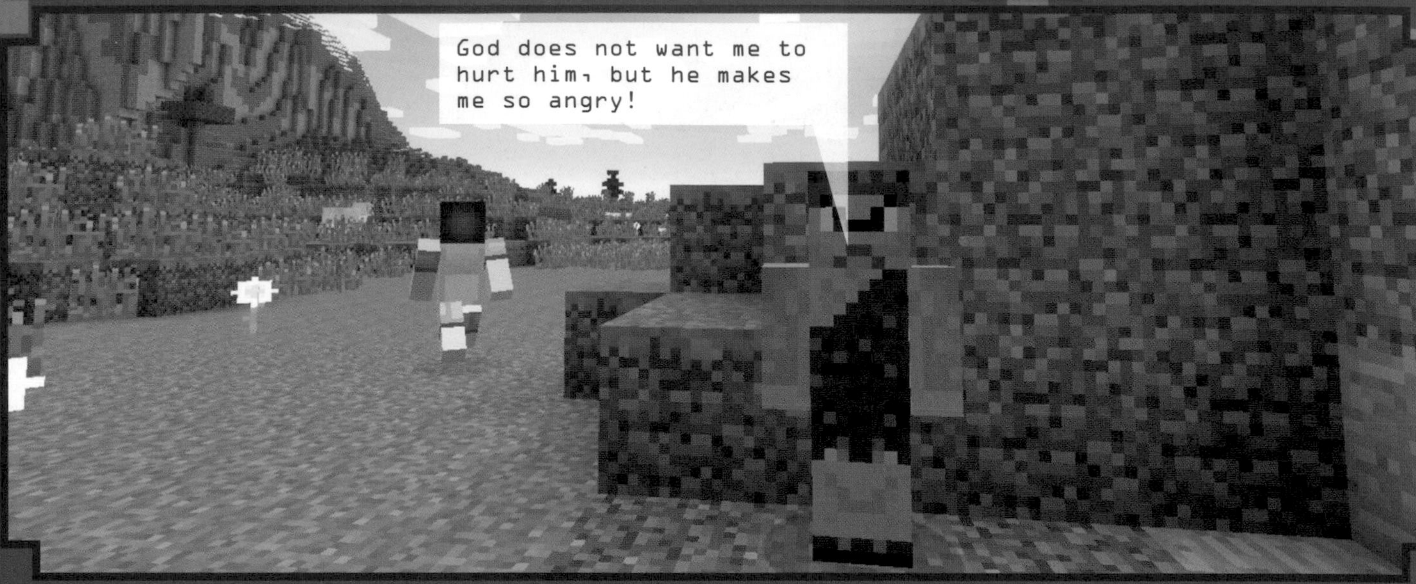
God does not want me to hurt him, but he makes me so angry!

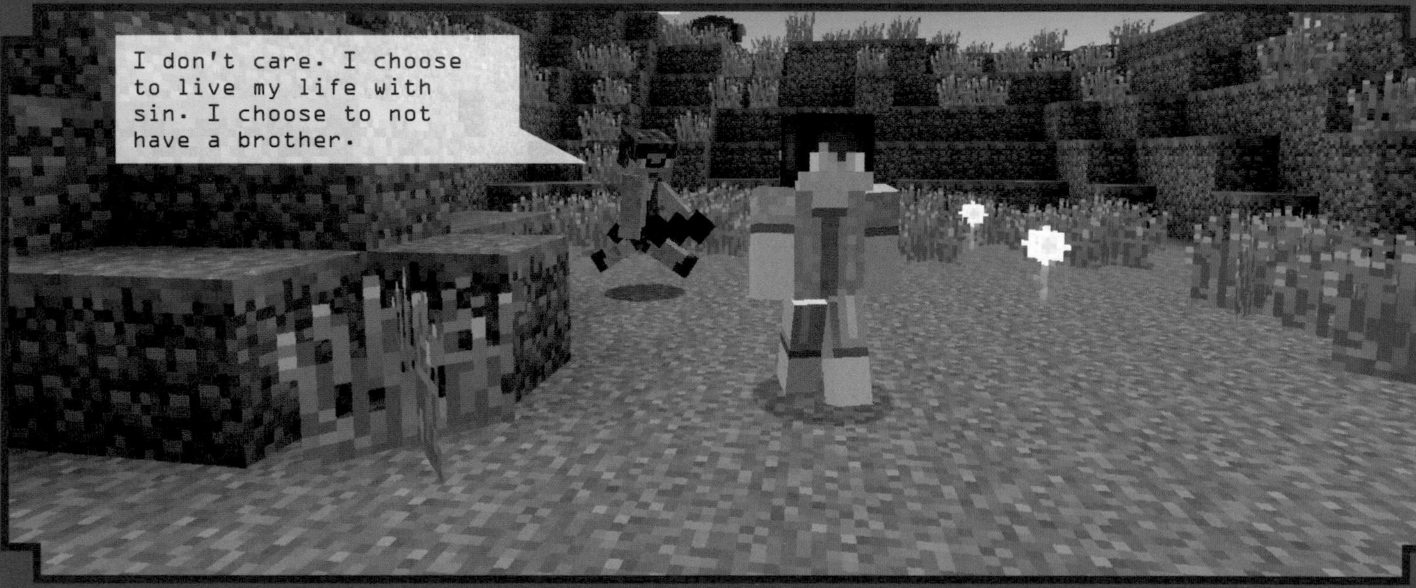
I don't care. I choose to live my life with sin. I choose to not have a brother.

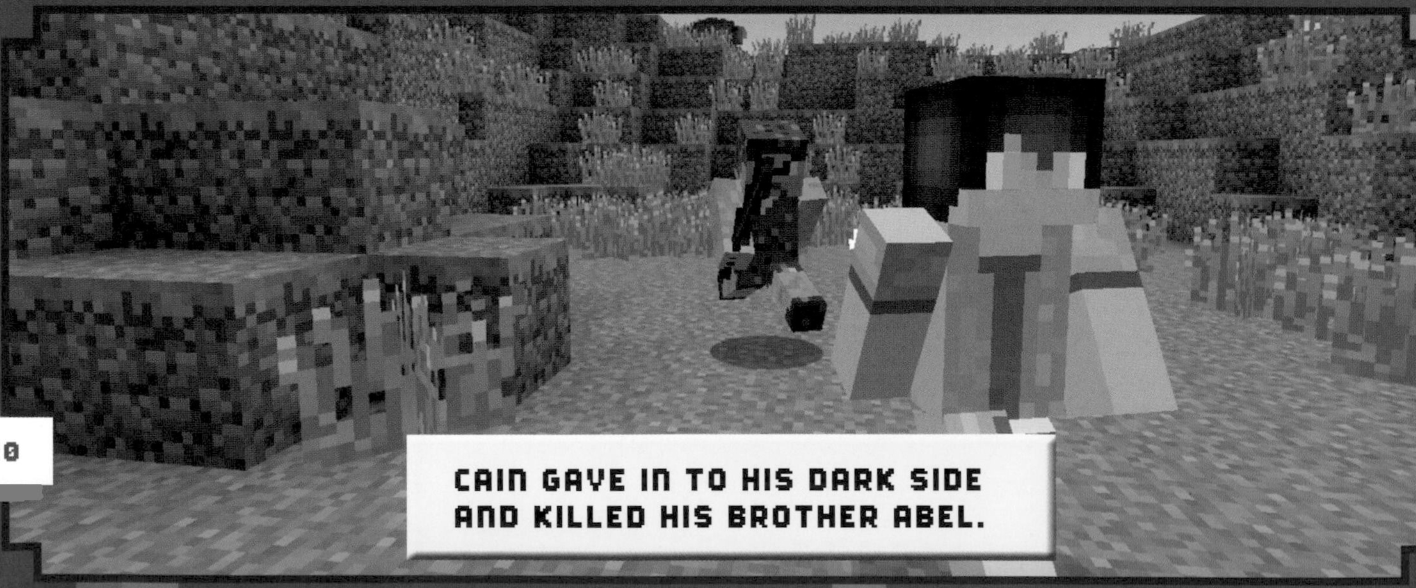
CAIN GAVE IN TO HIS DARK SIDE AND KILLED HIS BROTHER ABEL.

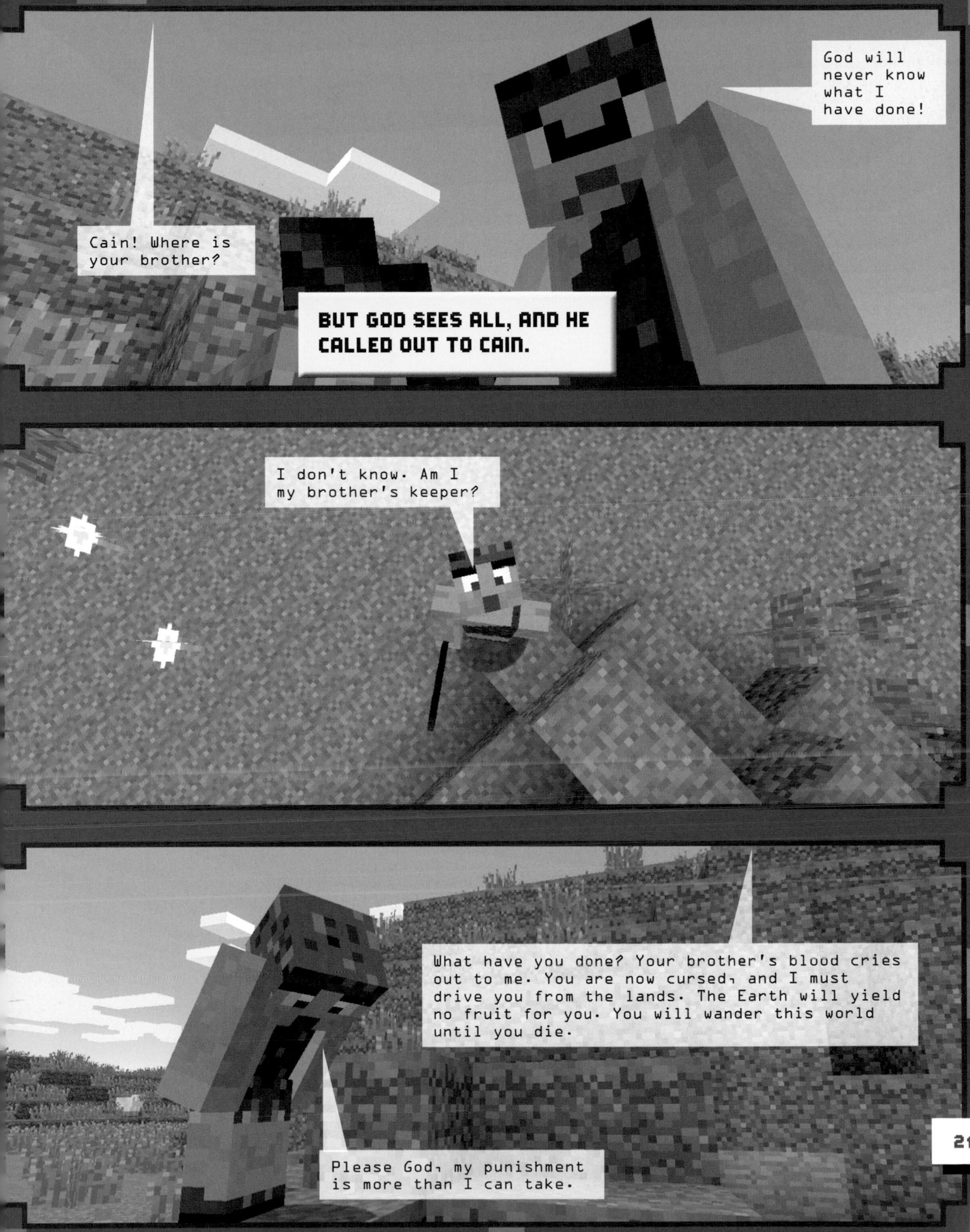
God will never know what I have done!
BUT GOD SEES ALL, AND HE CALLED OUT TO CAIN.
Cain! Where is your brother?
I don't know. Am I my brother's keeper?
What have you done? Your brother's blood cries out to me. You are now cursed, and I must drive you from the lands. The Earth will yield no fruit for you. You will wander this world until you die.
Please God, my punishment is more than I can take.

CAIN WANDERED FOR A LONG TIME. HE EVENTUALLY MARRIED AND HAD A SON NAMED ENOCH. ENOCH HAD CHILDREN, SO CAIN'S LEGACY WOULD CONTINUE.

ADAM AND EVE HAD ANOTHER SON, AND THEY NAMED HIM SETH.

God has granted us another child in place of our deceased son Abel.

NOAH AND THE
GREAT FLOOD

It looks like things on Earth are now a bit rocky. What happened?

Lord, I offer up my prayers and sacrifice to you. Guide me in all that I do.

FROM THE TIME OF ADAM, MAN HAD GROWN WICKED, AND THE LORD HAD BECOME SORRY HE HAD CREATED HIM. YET, AMONG ALL THE WICKED MEN OF THE EARTH WAS NOAH. HE WAS GOOD.

NOAH HAD THREE SONS: SHEM, HAM, AND JAPHETH. THEY, TOO, OBEYED THE LORD. GOD HAD A SPECIAL PLAN FOR NOAH, AS HE WOULD SOON SAVE ALL OF CREATION.

Oh Lord, grant me the ability to be truthful to all.

Lord, grant me wisdom.

Give me strength, so that I may serve you.

Noah, I have chosen you and your family to be saved. I will come to you in a dream, and in this dream, you will see what is to come. Follow My word and you will be saved.

WHEN NOAH WAS IN TOWN AMONG A THRONG OF PEOPLE, HE HEARD THE VOICE OF THE LORD.

Noah, you shall build an Ark, a boat big enough for all the creatures I shall send to you.

IN THE DREAM, GOD WARNED NOAH THAT A GREAT FLOOD WOULD SWEEP OVER THE EARTH BECAUSE OF MAN'S WICKEDNESS. GOD TOLD NOAH TO BUILD AN ARK. GOD WOULD THEN BRING ALL THE CREATURES OF THE LAND TO NOAH WHERE HE WOULD LOAD THEM ONTO THE ARK TO BE SAVED FROM THE FLOOD.

Looks like we're gonna need a bigger boat. I better get to work!

NOAH FOLLOWED GOD'S INSTRUCTIONS FOR HOW TO BUILD THE ARK. GOD SAID, "THE ARK IS TO BE MADE OF CYPRESS WOOD, WITH ROOMS IN IT AND COATED WITH PITCH INSIDE AND OUT. THE ARK IS TO BE 450 FEET LONG, 75 FEET WIDE, AND 45 FEET HIGH. IT IS TO HAVE A DOOR IN THE SIDE, WITH LOWER, MIDDLE, AND UPPER DECKS. TWO OF EVERY KIND OF BIRD, OF EVERY KIND OF ANIMAL, AND OF EVERY KIND OF CREATURE THAT MOVES ALONG THE GROUND WILL COME TO YOU TO BE KEPT ALIVE. YOU ARE TO TAKE EVERY KIND OF FOOD THAT IS TO BE EATEN AND STORE IT AWAY AS FOOD FOR YOU AND FOR THEM."

NOAH AND HIS FAMILY WORKED NONSTOP ON THE ARK. IN TIME, THE ARK HAD FORM AND SHAPE, AND SOON IT BECAME A BOAT.

Brothers, God has warned me that a flood is coming.

NOAH WARNED THE PEOPLE OF WHAT WAS TO COME, BUT THEY LOOKED TO THE SKY AND LAUGHED. THEY COULD NOT SEE GOD, AND SO THEY DID NOT BELIEVE IN HIM.

Lord, I am your faithful servant and have done as you have asked. The work is complete.

I have one more thing for you to do...

NOAH CONTINUED HIS WORK UNTIL THE TIME CAME WHEN THE ARK WAS READY.

Wow, now I understand why the Ark had to be so big.

NOAH THEN LOOKED OUT AND SAW A PARADE OF ANIMALS MAKING THEIR WAY TO THE ARK. THE ANIMALS CAME TWO AT A TIME; ONE MALE AND ONE FEMALE OF EACH ANIMAL WERE LED BY THE LORD TO NOAH.

I hope everyone is comfortable. This is going to be our home for a while.

IT TOOK SOME TIME, BUT ALL THE ANIMALS WERE LOADED ONTO THE ARK BY NOAH AND HIS FAMILY, AND THEN TENDED TO IN THEIR PENS.

29

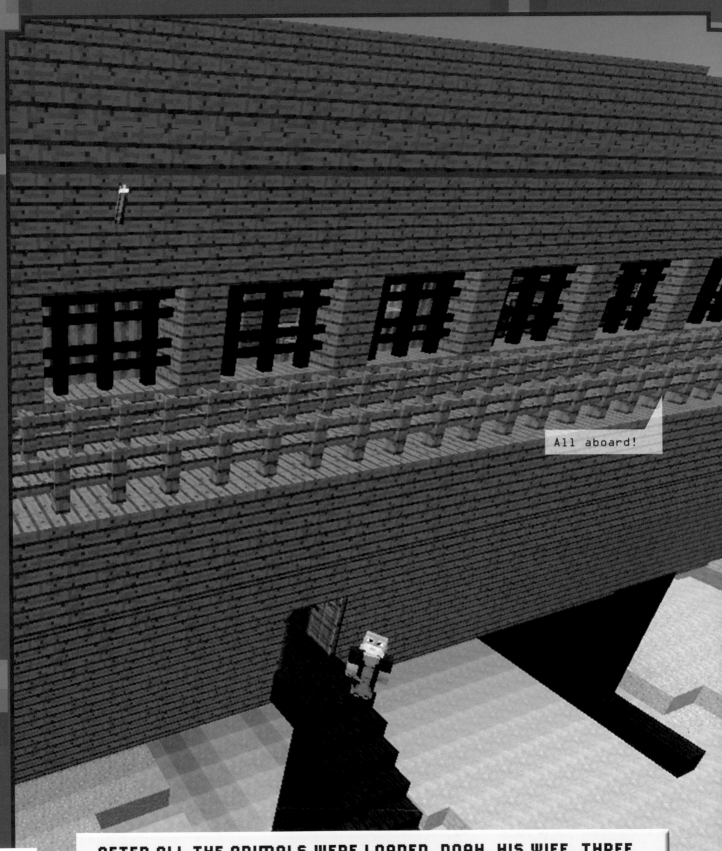

All aboard!

AFTER ALL THE ANIMALS WERE LOADED, NOAH, HIS WIFE, THREE SONS, AND THEIR WIVES ENTERED THE ARK. THEN THE DOOR WAS SHUT.

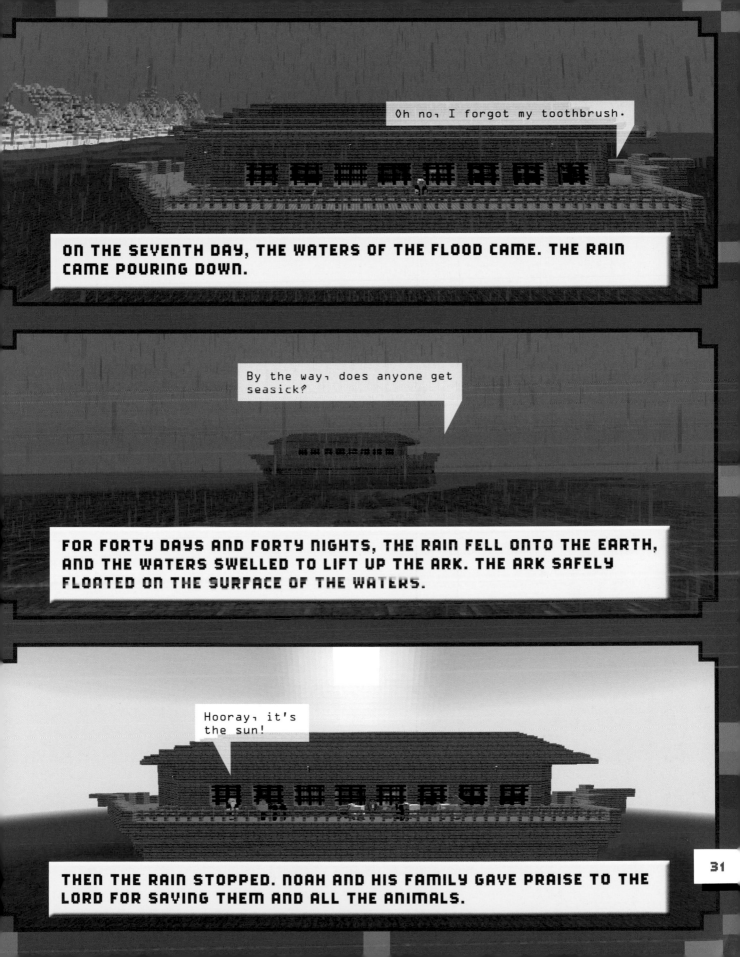

Oh no, I forgot my toothbrush.

ON THE SEVENTH DAY, THE WATERS OF THE FLOOD CAME. THE RAIN CAME POURING DOWN.

By the way, does anyone get seasick?

FOR FORTY DAYS AND FORTY NIGHTS, THE RAIN FELL ONTO THE EARTH, AND THE WATERS SWELLED TO LIFT UP THE ARK. THE ARK SAFELY FLOATED ON THE SURFACE OF THE WATERS.

Hooray, it's the sun!

31

THEN THE RAIN STOPPED. NOAH AND HIS FAMILY GAVE PRAISE TO THE LORD FOR SAVING THEM AND ALL THE ANIMALS.

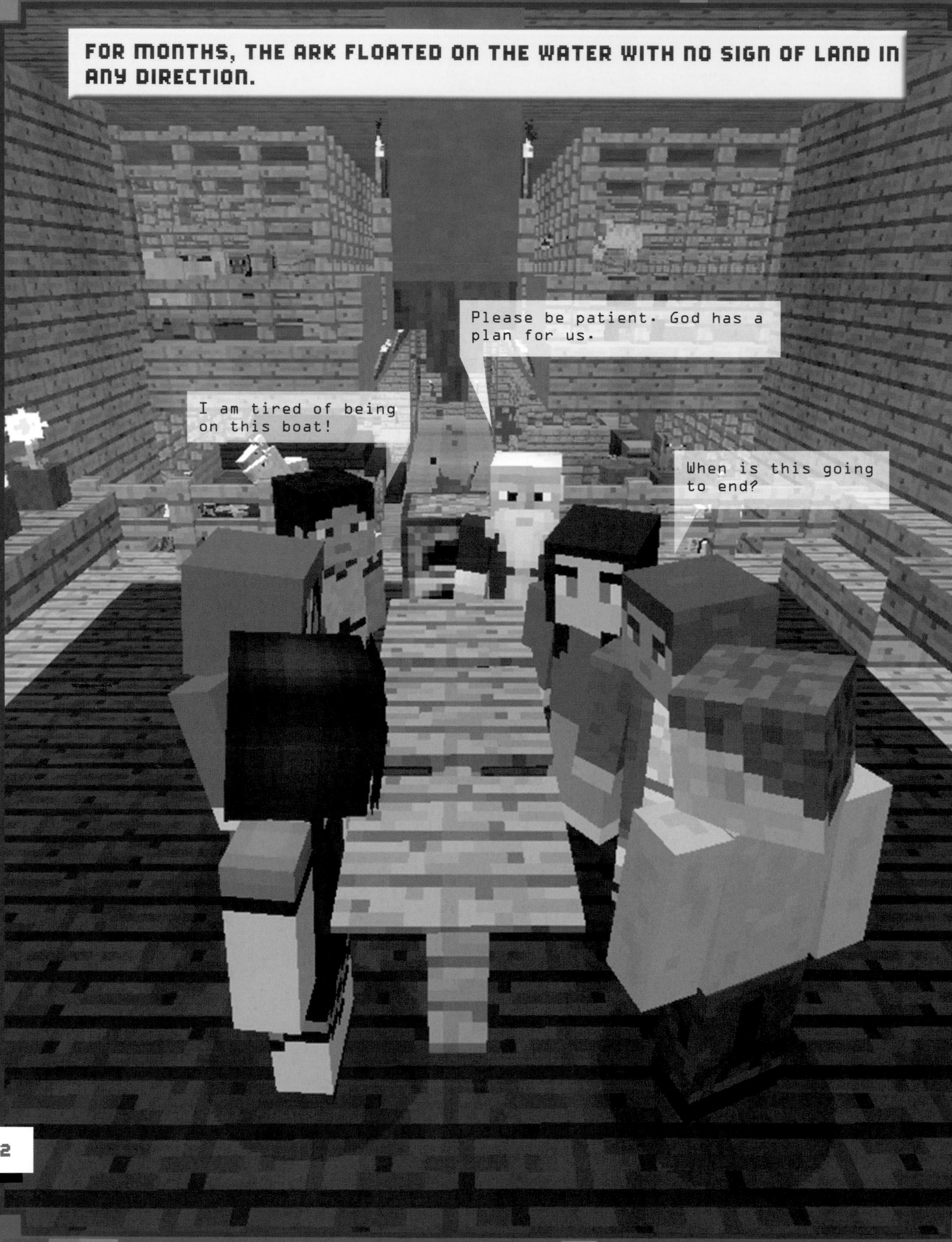
FOR MONTHS, THE ARK FLOATED ON THE WATER WITH NO SIGN OF LAND IN ANY DIRECTION.
I am tired of being on this boat!
Please be patient. God has a plan for us.
When is this going to end?

Have faith in Me.

I hope the waters will drop soon enough for land to appear.

FINALLY, THE WATERS BEGAN TO RECEDE. NOAH SENT A RAVEN AND A DOVE OUT TO FIND DRY LAND. THE BIRDS RETURNED TO THE ARK WITH NOTHING, WHICH WAS A SIGN THAT THE EARTH WAS STILL COVERED IN WATER.

WEEKS PASSED, BUT NOAH AND HIS FAMILY DID NOT LOSE HOPE. NOAH SENT OUT THE BIRDS AGAIN AND AGAIN, BUT EACH TIME THEY WOULD COME BACK WITH NOTHING. FINALLY, NOAH TRIED ONE MORE TIME. HE PRAYED TO THE LORD THAT LAND WOULD BE FOUND. NOAH'S HEART BEGAN TO SINK WHEN HE REALIZED THE DOVE HAD PLUCKED A NEWLY GROWN OLIVE BRANCH AND BROUGHT IT BACK TO HIM. THIS WAS THE SIGN THAT THE EARTH WAS DRY AND LIFE COULD BEGIN AGAIN.

Come out of the Ark, you and your wife, your sons and their wives. Bring out every living creature that is with you. Let them roam free on the Earth so that they may be fruitful and increase in numbers. Life shall begin again.

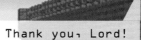

Thank you, Lord!

THE ARK RAN AGROUND ON DRY LAND, AND THE WATERS RECEDED AROUND IT.

35

NOAH WAS GRATEFUL TO THE LORD FOR SAVING HIM AND HIS FAMILY. HE BUILT AN ALTAR AND WORSHIPED THE LORD.

GOD PROMISED THAT HE WOULD NEVER AGAIN SEND A FLOOD TO JUDGE THE SINS OF MAN. THEN GOD SHOWED NOAH A RAINBOW, AND TOLD NOAH THAT THIS WAS THE SIGN OF HIS PROMISE TO ALL MANKIND.

TOWER OF BABEL

They are trying to build physical structures to reach Me.

But You are reached by going within oneself.

ONCE UPON A TIME, ALL THE WORLD SPOKE A SINGLE LANGUAGE AND USED THE SAME WORDS. AS MEN MOVED TOWARD THE EAST, THEY CAME ACROSS A GREAT PLAIN IN THE LANDS OF SHINAR AND SETTLED THERE. THEY SAID TO EACH OTHER, "COME, LET US MAKE A TOWER. WE WILL REACH THE HEAVENS."

THE LORD BECAME WORRIED THAT MAN WOULD GROW WICKED ONCE MORE. SO THE LORD CONFUSED THEIR SPEECH. THIS IS WHY IT IS CALLED TOWER OF BABEL, FOR WORKERS COULD NOT UNDERSTAND WHAT THE OTHERS WERE SAYING.

THOSE WHO SPOKE ONE LANGUAGE MOVED AWAY FROM THE OTHERS WHO SPOKE DIFFERENTLY. MAN DISPERSED ACROSS THE EARTH.

GOD CALLS ABRAHAM

I have selected which group will be the Chosen People to carry on My work on Earth.

Abram, I call to you. Leave your own country, take your relatives, and go to a country that I will show you.

I do not understand why you have commanded me to do this, but I trust in You, Lord and will do as You have said.

THIS IS THE STORY OF ABRAHAM. THE LORD BEGAN HIS PLAN TO BRING MAN BACK TO SALVATION, AND IT WAS TO START WITH ABRAHAM. IN THE BEGINNING, ABRAHAM WAS CALLED ABRAM. ABRAM, LIKE NOAH, FOLLOWED AND LOVED GOD.

There it is, Canaan! Let's continue to follow Abram.

Let us enter the land and set down roots to begin a new life.

SO ABRAM OBEYED THE LORD AS HE LED THEM TO THE LAND KNOWN AS CANAAN. ABRAM'S WIFE, SARAI, AND HIS NEPHEW, LOT, CAME ALONG.

We have done well in such a short time, Lot. We should count our stock.

It may be hard. They keep moving!

42

IN THE LAND OF CANAAN, THE LORD BLESSED ABRAM AND HIS NEPHEW, LOT. ABRAM AND LOT WORKED HARD AND BECAME RICH. SOON, ABRAM AND LOT'S HERDS BECAME SO NUMEROUS THEY COULD NOT BE COUNTED.

TIME PASSED, AND THE HERDS GREW EVEN LARGER. ABRAM AND LOT'S CATTLE BECAME SO NUMEROUS THAT THE LAND COULD NOT SUPPORT BOTH TOGETHER, AND THEIR HERDSMEN BEGAN TO FIGHT OVER TERRITORY. ABRAM SAW THE FIGHTING AND WISHED FOR PEACE, SO HE CALLED LOT TO HIM. TOGETHER, THEY CAME UP WITH A PLAN.

LOT LOOKED OUT ONTO A GREAT PLAIN WHERE TWO CITIES SAT IN THE DISTANCE. THE CITIES WERE CALLED SODOM AND GOMORRAH. LOT AND HIS FAMILY FOUND THEIR WAY TO SODOM.

Abram, once again, you must move—this time, by your own choice. But I have not forgotten My covenant with you. I shall give all the lands of Canaan to you and your children and all their descendants forever. Also, from now on, you will be known as Abraham, which means "Exalted Father," and your wife will be Sarah.

GOD ONCE AGAIN SPOKE TO ABRAM.

What do you mean by "Exalted Father," and that the lands will belong to my children and their children's children? I am too old to have children.

ABRAHAM WAITED, BUT GOD DID NOT ANSWER. SO ABRAHAM WAS LEFT TO WONDER WHAT MIRACLE GOD WOULD PERFORM TO KEEP HIS PROMISE.

ABRAHAM DID AS GOD INSTRUCTED AND MADE HIS NEW HOME IN THE LANDS OF CANAAN. HE NEVER FORGOT GOD'S PROMISE, ALTHOUGH HE STILL WONDERED HOW IT WOULD BE FULFILLED.

THEN ONE DAY, SARAH CAME TO HIM WITH NEWS.

A SON WAS BORN, AND THEY NAMED HIM ISAAC.

SODOM AND GOMORRAH

Uh, God?

Yes, Gabriel.

Looks like there's some more cleansing that has to be done.

WHILE ABRAHAM LIVED IN THE LANDS OF CANAAN, HIS NEPHEW, LOT, RESIDED IN THE CITY OF SODOM.

SODOM HAD BECOME A BAD CITY. IN ORDER FOR CANAAN TO BE SAFE FOR ABRAHAM AND HIS DESCENDANTS, GOD WOULD HAVE TO STOP THE WICKEDNESS.

49

Please listen. You need to treat each other with kindness.

God shmod!

Blah, blah, blah, I have heard it all before.

ABRAHAM AND LOT TRIED TO TEACH THE PEOPLE OF SODOM AND GOMORRAH RIGHT FROM WRONG, BUT THEY WOULD NOT LISTEN. THEY TRIED TO HURT LOT AND ABRAHAM.

THE TIME FINALLY CAME WHEN GOD COULD NO LONGER STAND THESE TWO CITIES. IT WAS A QUIET NIGHT, AND LOT WENT TO HIS ROOF.

God, what should I do to save my family from this evil?

Move your family away from Sodom, for I will destroy this evil.

Say whatever you wish, but I am not going out there to live in tents and sleep among the animals.

LOT WARNED PEOPLE TO LEAVE, BUT NONE WOULD LISTEN. LOT'S TWO DAUGHTERS WANTED TO LEAVE, BUT THEIR HUSBANDS REFUSED TO GO. THEY DID NOT BELIEVE IN THE LORD.

LOT AND HIS TWO DAUGHTERS WERE THE ONLY ONES TO MAKE IT SAFELY OUT, FOR GOD HAD SENT FIRE AND BRIMSTONE TO DESTROY THE CITIES OF SODOM AND GOMORRAH.

A WIFE FOR ISAAC

TIME PASSED, AND ABRAHAM BECAME OLD. HIS SON, ISAAC, HAD GROWN TO BE A GODLY MAN.

BUT ISAAC WAS LONELY.

Poor Isaac, if only he had a wife to love him.

ABRAHAM CALLED TO HIS MOST TRUSTED SERVANT.

I have a great task for you!

Go to the lands of my father and find my son a wife.

But what if I am not able to find him a wife?

The Lord will send his angel ahead of you so that you can find her.

THE SERVANT OF ABRAHAM LOADED UP HIS ANIMALS WITH A VARIETY OF GOODS AND SUPPLIES BECAUSE THEY WOULD TRAVEL FAR TO FIND ISAAC'S WIFE.

HE ARRIVED AT THE BIGGEST CITY HE HAD EVER SEEN.

Oh Lord, this place is so big and there are so many people. I do not know how I will find a wife for Isaac.

Lord, let this be the test: If the first woman I ask gives water to me and my animals, she will be Isaac's wife.

THE SERVANT TOOK HIS ANIMALS TO A WELL TO DRINK WATER. MANY WOMEN WERE THERE. HE SPOKE WITH GOD.

Would you like a drink?

Uh, yes. Thank you.

THE SERVANT APPROACHED A WOMAN DRESSED IN PURPLE WHOSE NAME, HE LATER LEARNED, WAS REBEKAH. REBEKAH WAS SO VERY KIND THAT SHE DIDN'T EVEN WAIT FOR HIM TO ASK.

I will also water your animals.

Groat!

Praise the Lord, for He has provided Isaac a wife!

55

THE SERVANT TOOK OUT A GOLD NOSE RING AND TWO GOLD BRACELETS. HE GAVE THEM TO REBEKAH.

What is your name and who is your father?

My name is Rebekah, and I am the daughter of Bethuel.

We have plenty of room in our house if you would like to rest.

You are very kind. It is you I have come to find. Please take me to your father.

SO THE SERVANT WENT TO THE HOUSE OF BETHUEL TO SPEAK TO REBEKAH'S FATHER.

I have come to ask for Rebekah to marry my master's son, Isaac.

Do as the Lord wills.

I will miss you all, but I look forward to meeting my new husband.

THE NEXT MORNING, REBEKAH AND THE SERVANT PREPARED TO LEAVE.

What will Isaac be like?

He is strong, tall, and handsome. He is kind and loving to all. But most important, he is a godly man.

AFTER MANY DAYS OF TRAVEL, THE CARAVAN REACHED THE LANDS OF CANAAN.

Who is this man in the field? He is very handsome.

That is Isaac.

THE SERVANT INTRODUCED THEM. ISAAC LED REBEKAH INTO A TENT.

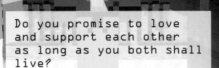

Do you promise to love
and support each other
as long as you both shall
live?

SO SHE BECAME HIS WIFE AND ISAAC LOVED HER. THEY LIVED THE REST
OF THEIR DAYS TOGETHER, HAPPY WITH GOD'S BLESSING.

JACOB AND ESAU

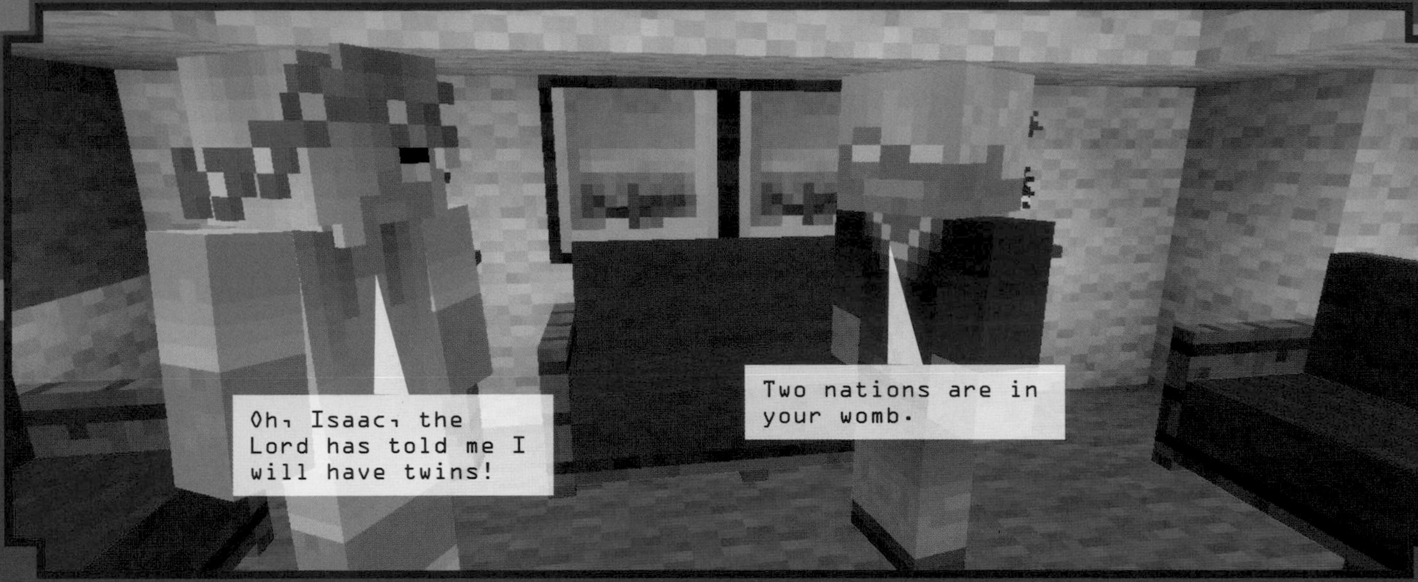
Oh, Isaac, the Lord has told me I will have twins!
Two nations are in your womb.

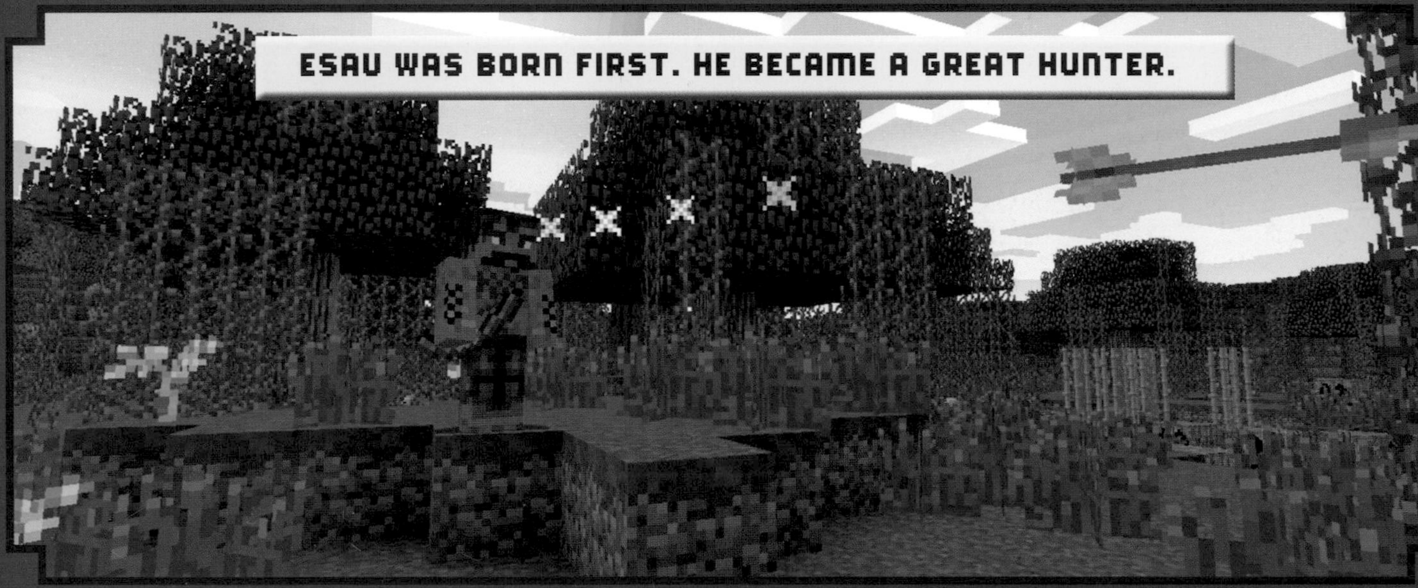
ESAU WAS BORN FIRST. HE BECAME A GREAT HUNTER.

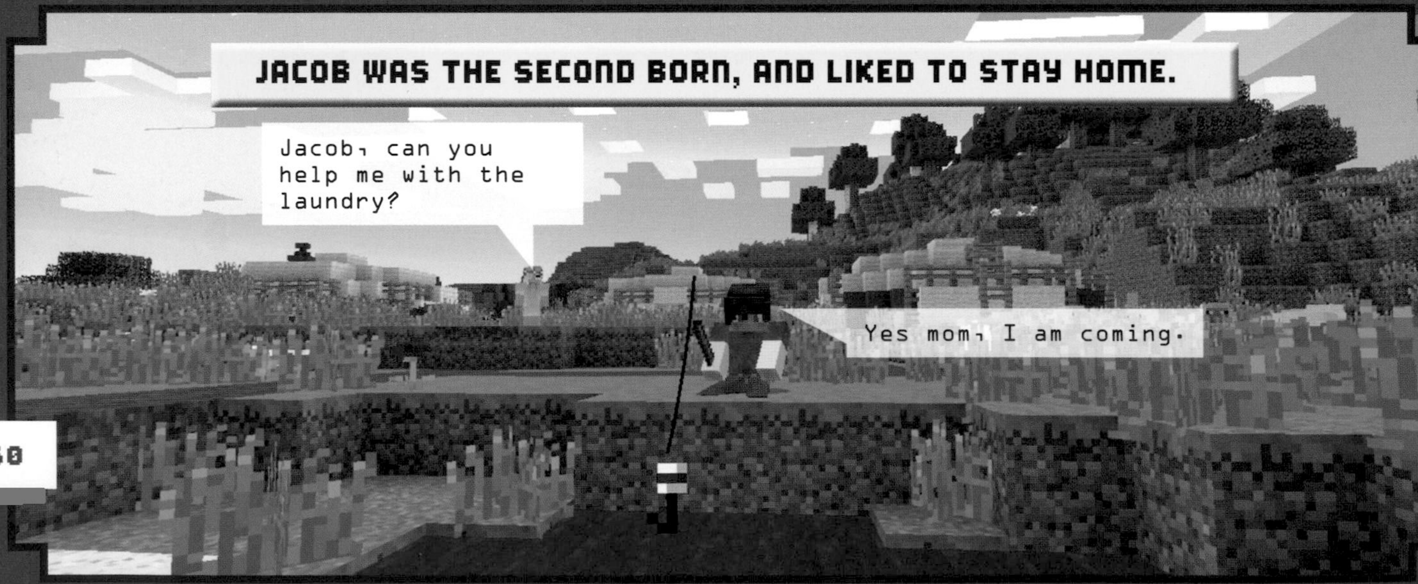
JACOB WAS THE SECOND BORN, AND LIKED TO STAY HOME.
Jacob, can you help me with the laundry?
Yes mom, I am coming.

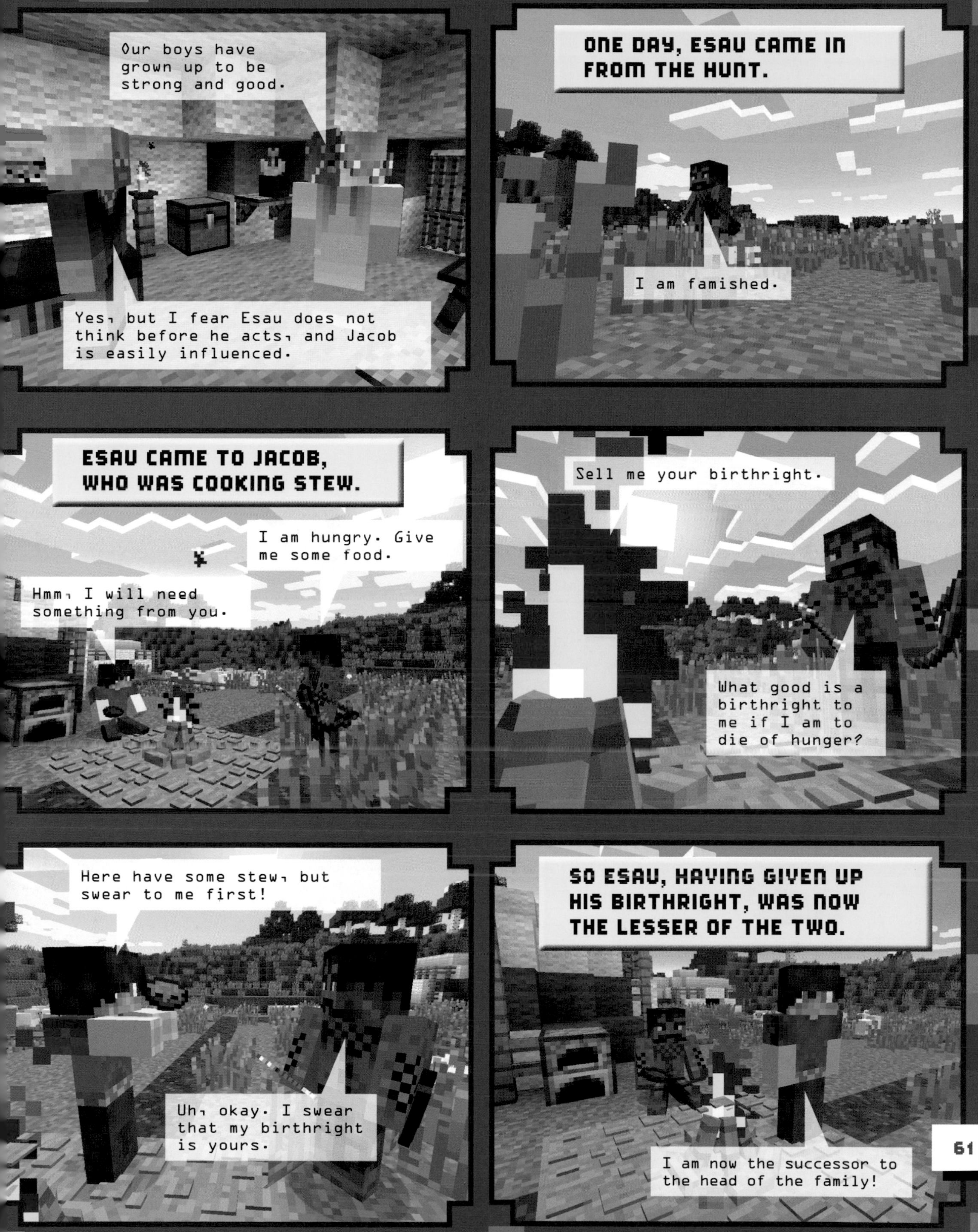
Our boys have grown up to be strong and good.
Yes, but I fear Esau does not think before he acts, and Jacob is easily influenced.
ONE DAY, ESAU CAME IN FROM THE HUNT.
I am famished.
ESAU CAME TO JACOB, WHO WAS COOKING STEW.
I am hungry. Give me some food.
Hmm, I will need something from you.
Sell me your birthright.
What good is a birthright to me if I am to die of hunger?
Here have some stew, but swear to me first!
Uh, okay. I swear that my birthright is yours.
SO ESAU, HAVING GIVEN UP HIS BIRTHRIGHT, WAS NOW THE LESSER OF THE TWO.
I am now the successor to the head of the family!

Esau, my son, the time has come to pass on the leadership of the family to you. But first, go and hunt, for we are running low on spiced meats and jackrabbit haunches.

I must speak to Jacob.

Jacob, I have a plan that will get you Esau's blessing directly from Isaac.

OK, mom!

Isaac is hungry. Quickly, go to the flock and bring me two goats.

This will trick Isaac.

REBEKAH PREPARED THE GOATS SO THAT JACOB COULD GIVE IT TO ISAAC.

Pretend that you are Esau and give this meat to Isaac. He will bless you instead of Esau.

But mother, Esau is very hairy.

REBEKAH GAVE JACOB THE PREPARED MEATS AND COVERED HIS ARMS AND NECK WITH GOAT HAIR.

ISAAC COULD NOT SEE BECAUSE OF HIS OLD AGE AND HE COULD NOT TELL WHO WAS ENTERING THE TENT.

It is Esau, father. I am here to satisfy your hunger.

Who is that? It sounds like Jacob.

Come here so I may touch you.

You sound like Jacob, but feel like Esau.

Thank you. It is now time for me to bless you: May God give you all things. May the nations of the world serve you.

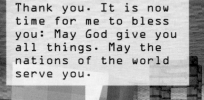

Father, I have returned.

Esau? Oh no! What have I done? I'm sorry, but I have just given my blessing to Jacob!

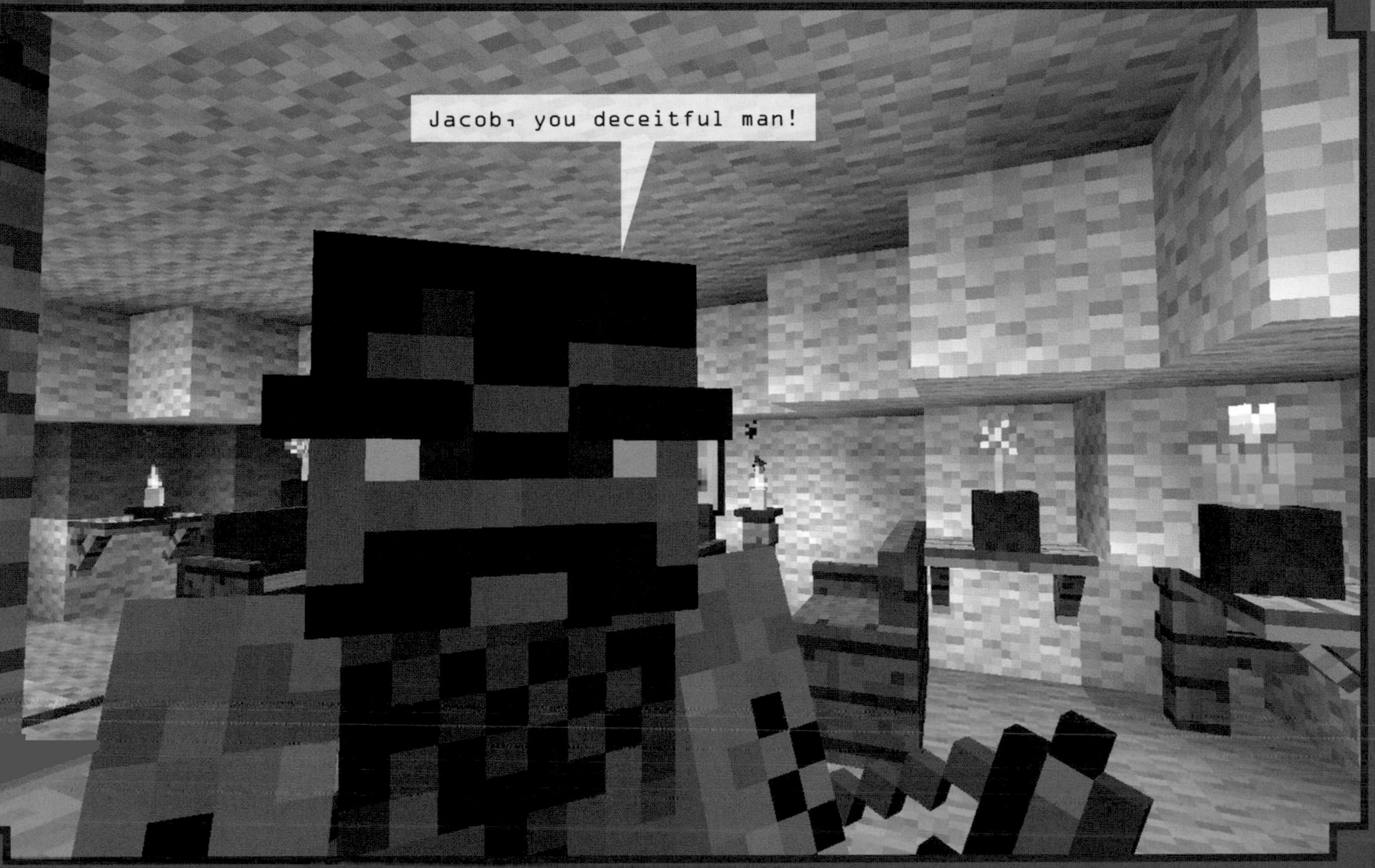
Jacob, you deceitful man!

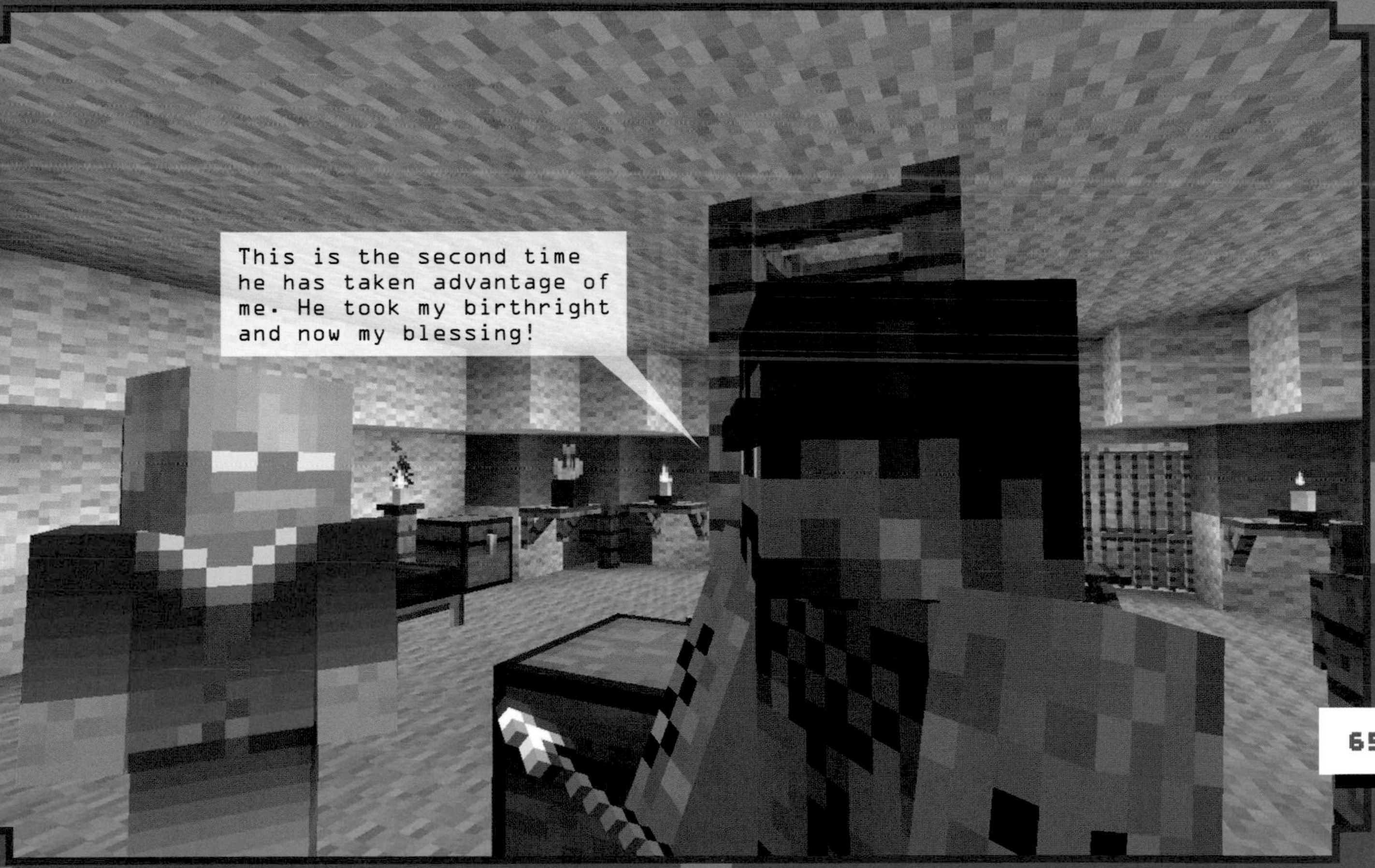
This is the second time he has taken advantage of me. He took my birthright and now my blessing!

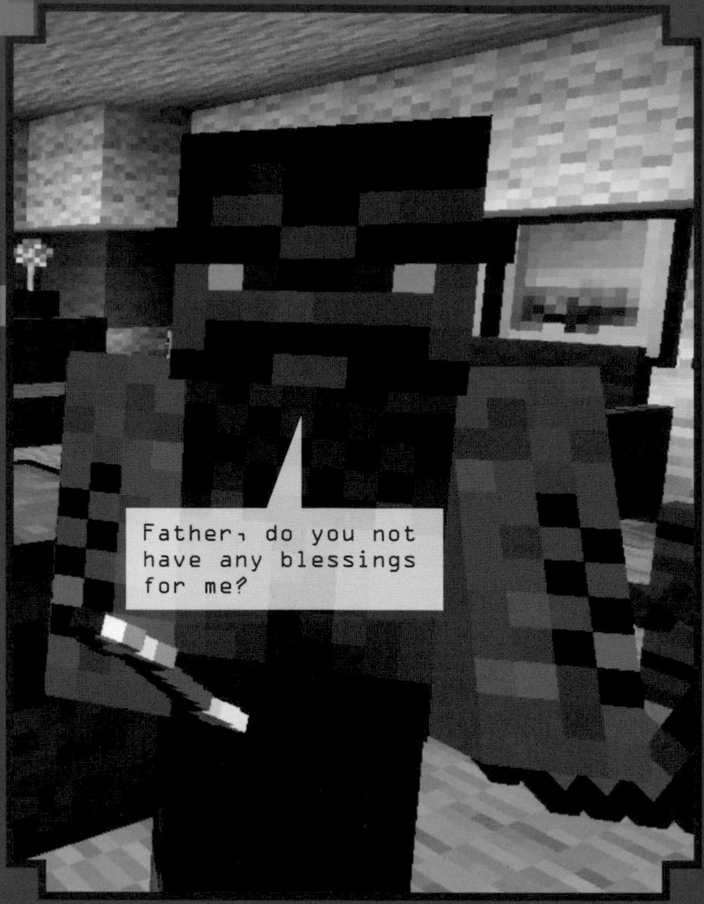
Father, do you not have any blessings for me?
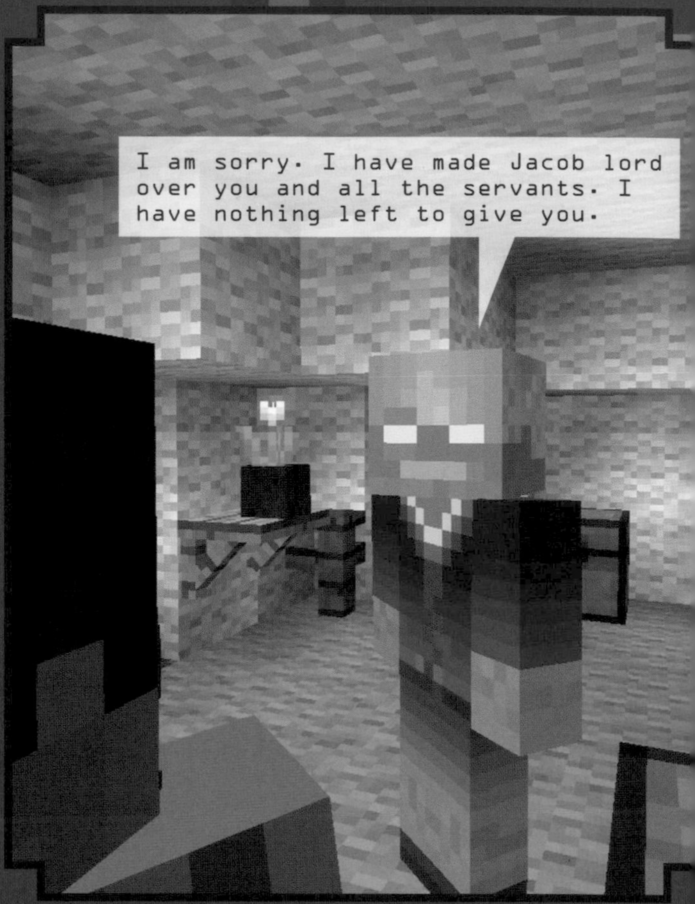
I am sorry. I have made Jacob lord over you and all the servants. I have nothing left to give you.
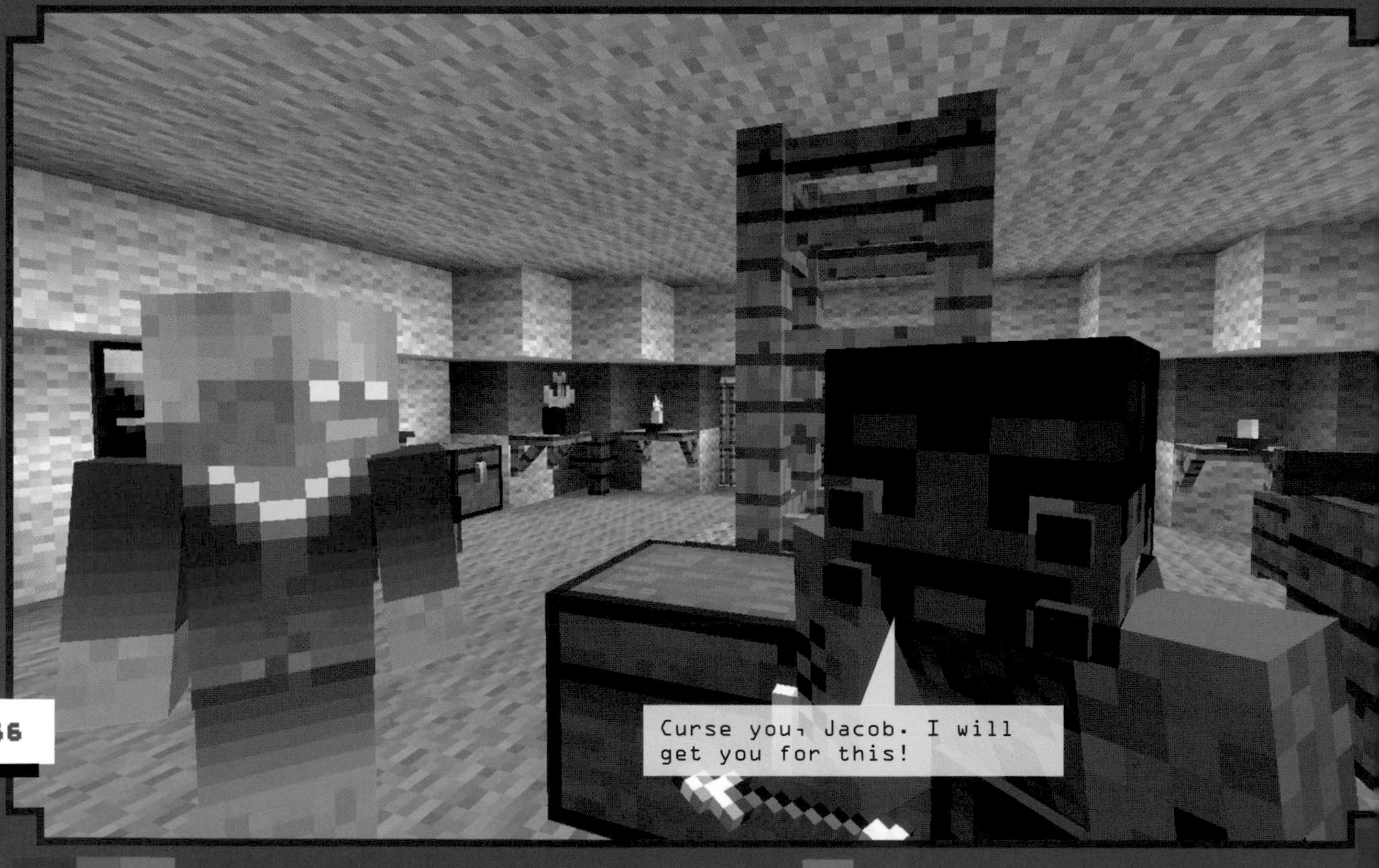
Curse you, Jacob. I will get you for this!

STAIRWAY TO HEAVEN

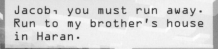

Jacob, you must run away. Run to my brother's house in Haran.

Oh, no! Bring Jacob to me.

Rebekah, Esau has sworn to get rid of Jacob.

I will miss you.

I will send for you when your brother's temper cools and he forgets.

JACOB LEFT HIS HOME AND ALL HE KNEW. HE HEADED OFF INTO THE WILD TO FIND SAFETY IN HARAN.

BY NIGHTFALL, JACOB DECIDED TO REST. WHILE HE SLEPT, HE DREAMED OF FANTASTIC VISIONS ABOVE HIM.

I will give you and your kinfolk the land on which you lay.

I am the Lord, the God of your fathers Abraham and Isaac.

THEN JACOB SAW ANGELS DESCEND A STAIRWAY THAT LED TO HEAVEN.

THE NEXT MORNING, JACOB REMEMBERED HIS DREAM.
Surely the Lord is in this place.
How holy are these blocks? This must be the portal to the house of God, the gate to heaven!
JACOB TOOK STONES AND MADE A PILLAR. HE POURED OIL ON TOP OF IT AND GAVE THANKS.
JACOB THEN MADE A PROMISE TO GOD.
If God will be with me and will always watch over me, I will give Him one-tenth of all He provides.

JACOB AND HIS WIFE

There is a well and shepherds. I will go talk to them.

JACOB CONTINUED ON HIS JOURNEY UNTIL HE FINALLY CAME TO HARAN.

Greetings, my brother. Do you know where the house of Laban is?

Yes, this is his land and that woman over there is his daughter, Rachel.

JACOB APPROACHED RACHEL.

You are so kind, but I have all I need, thank you.

My name is Jacob. May I help you collect water?

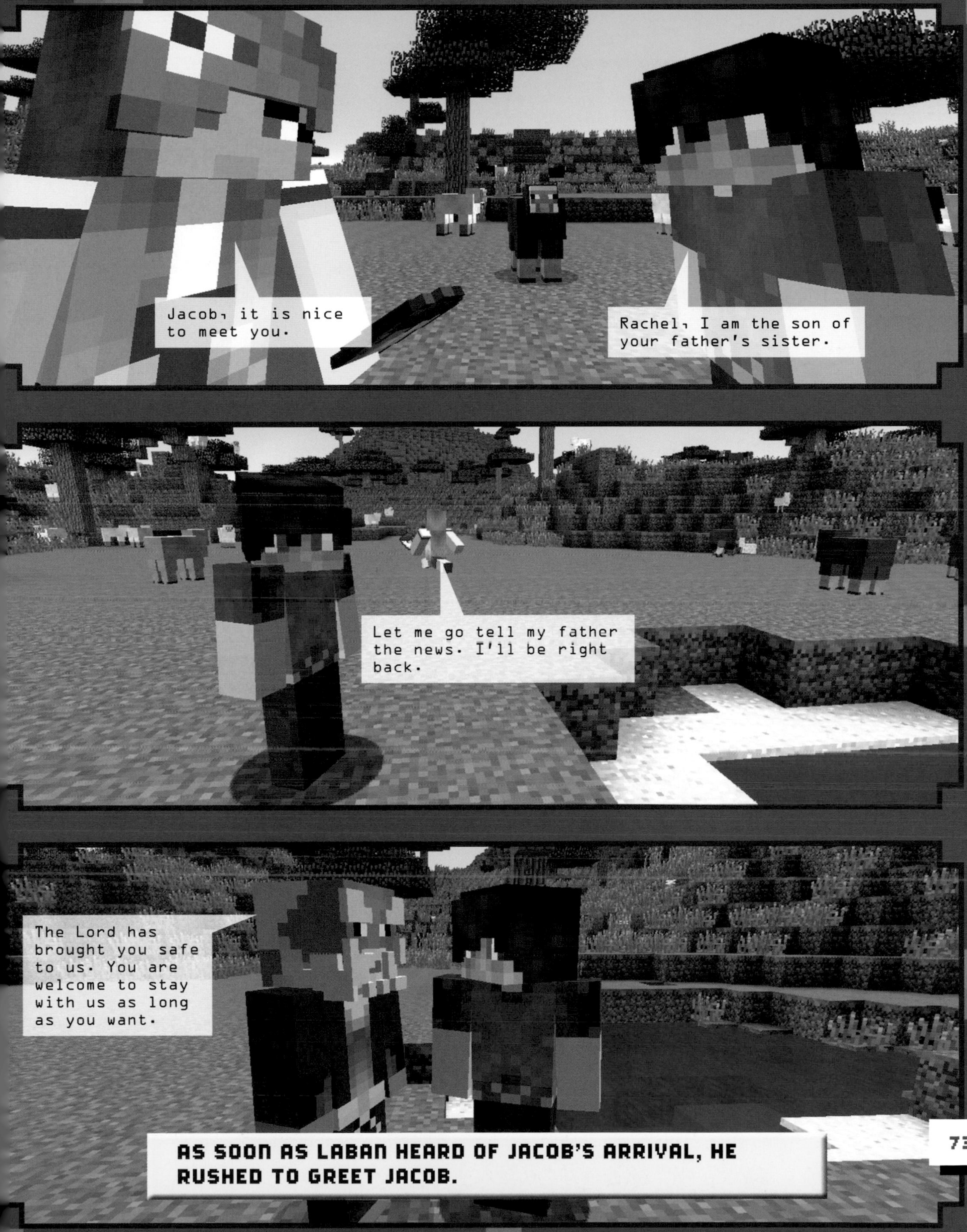
Jacob, it is nice to meet you.
Rachel, I am the son of your father's sister.
Let me go tell my father the news. I'll be right back.
AS SOON AS LABAN HEARD OF JACOB'S ARRIVAL, HE RUSHED TO GREET JACOB.
The Lord has brought you safe to us. You are welcome to stay with us as long as you want.

AFTER JACOB HAD BEEN WITH LABAN AND HIS FAMILY FOR A WHOLE MONTH, LABAN CAME TO JACOB.

The time has come for you to earn your keep. You will work for me, but I will pay your price.

LABAN HAD TWO DAUGHTERS. THE OLDEST WAS NAMED LEAH, WHOM NO MAN WANTED, AND THE YOUNGER DAUGHTER, RACHEL, WAS LOVELY AND DESIRED BY MANY MEN.

I will work for you on the condition that I may marry Rachel.

First, you must prove to me your loyalty. You may wed Rachel after seven years of laboring in my fields.

My years of hard work are complete. I am ready to wed Rachel as promised.

JACOB AGREED AND SERVED HIS SEVEN YEARS TO EARN RACHEL AS HIS WIFE.

SO LABAN GATHERED ALL THE PEOPLE FOR THE FEAST.

My friends, my family, I bring you together on this very special day. Let us celebrate!

I now pronounce you husband and wife.

I have waited seven years for this moment.

THE TIME CAME FOR JACOB TO SEE HIS WIFE. HE LIFTED THE VEIL.

What! You are not Rachel! You are Leah. I was tricked!

JACOB WAS FURIOUS THAT HE HAD BEEN TRICKED INTO MARRYING RACHEL'S SISTER LEAH.

JACOB CONFRONTED LABAN.

It is our custom to give the first daughter in marriage. Marry Leah and work another seven years and then you can wed Rachel.

Rachel is the one I love, so I have no choice. I will work for you for seven more years, but then I must leave this place.

LABAN ONCE AGAIN PROMISED RACHEL TO JACOB.

Time will pass by quickly, you'll see.

But we must wait so long.

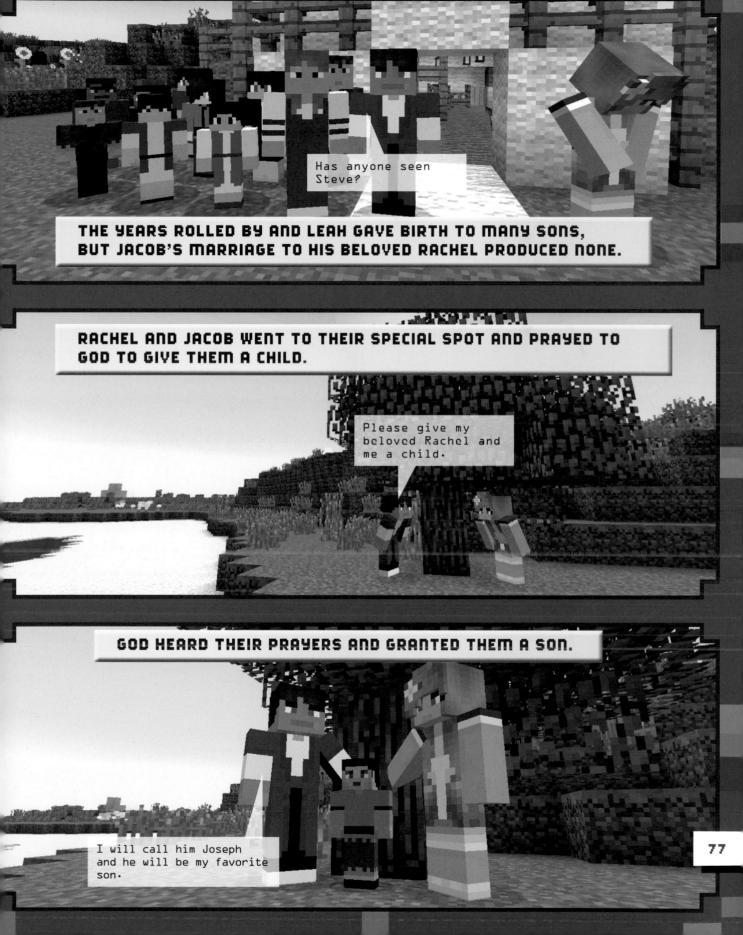

Has anyone seen Steve?

THE YEARS ROLLED BY AND LEAH GAVE BIRTH TO MANY SONS, BUT JACOB'S MARRIAGE TO HIS BELOVED RACHEL PRODUCED NONE.

RACHEL AND JACOB WENT TO THEIR SPECIAL SPOT AND PRAYED TO GOD TO GIVE THEM A CHILD.

Please give my beloved Rachel and me a child.

GOD HEARD THEIR PRAYERS AND GRANTED THEM A SON.

I will call him Joseph and he will be my favorite son.

77

JACOB RETURNS HOME

THE TIME CAME FOR JACOB TO RETURN HOME. HE TRAVELLED WITH A CARAVAN OF HIS FOUR WIVES AND ELEVEN CHILDREN.

AT THE FRONT OF THE CARAVAN WAS JOSEPH, JACOB'S FAVORITE SON.

Now Joseph, God has a special plan for us. God loves us, and that is why we are returning to our homeland.

God, You have said to me, "I will surely make you prosper and will make your descendants like the sand of the sea." I have learned from You that what I did to my brother, Esau, was wrong. Please allow him to forgive me.

AS JACOB APPROACHED CANAAN, HE STOPPED AND PRAYED TO GOD.

WHILE JACOB WAS ALONE IN HIS PRAYERS, A MYSTERIOUS MAN CAME TO HIM AND BEGAN TO WRESTLE WITH HIM.

Let me go.

No, tell me you bless me!

THE TWO JOSTLED THEIR BODIES UNTIL NEARLY DAWN, WHEN JACOB SEIZED THE UPPER HAND AND WON.

JACOB HAD WRESTLED WITH GOD AND FOUND FAVOR.

You have changed and grown to be a good man, or else you wouldn't have bested My messenger. Your line shall be the line of My covenant.

THE SUN ROSE AND JACOB LIMPED BACK TO JOIN HIS FAMILY.

Jacob, you are limping.

I am okay, for the Lord has blessed me.

Jacob, your brother comes, and he comes with four hundred men.

JACOB LOOKED UP TO SEE A SERVANT APPROACH.

JACOB BRAVELY WENT ON AHEAD OF HIS FAMILY TO MEET HIS BROTHER.

My dearest brother, welcome home.

My brother, I return humbly to you and father!

ESAU JUMPED FROM HIS HORSE AND RAN TO MEET JACOB. THEY EMBRACED.

TEARS OF JOY STREAMED DOWN THEIR FACES.

I have missed you! Please forgive me!

Forgiveness is not needed. You will always be my brother.

JACOB AND ESAU SAID THEIR GOODBYES.

JACOB CONTINUED ON HIS WAY TO SEE HIS FATHER ISAAC.

ALONG THE WAY, RACHEL WENT INTO LABOR WITH ANOTHER CHILD.

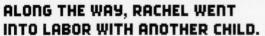

Jacob, we have to stop. The baby is coming and I can't hold out any longer.

JACOB WAITED ANXIOUSLY OUTSIDE OF RACHEL'S TENT, PRAYING FOR GOD'S GOOD WILL WHILE SHE DELIVERED THE BABY.

Master, you have a son, but Rachel's spirit has moved on to sit beside our Lord.

We are blessed and cursed! But I know God has a plan. We shall name the new child Benjamin—it's a strong name, and we need to be strong in this world. Now only he and you remind me of my true love.

JACOB NAMED THE PLACE WHERE RACHEL WAS BURIED BETHLEHEM.

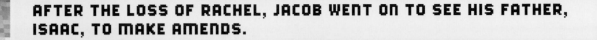

AFTER THE LOSS OF RACHEL, JACOB WENT ON TO SEE HIS FATHER, ISAAC, TO MAKE AMENDS.

Forgive me, father, for I have sinned against you and God.

ISAAC'S FRAGILE HEALTH AND ADVANCED AGE CONFINED HIM TO HIS BED.

I weep with joy at your return.

God has forgiven me, and I have learned to be an honest man.

I forgive you, my son. Thanks be to God for your return. I prayed to live long enough to see you again.

AFTER SAYING THESE WORDS, ISAAC EXHALED HIS LAST BREATH.

JOSEPH HELPED JACOB BURY HIS FATHER.

I have learned to be a godly man, father. I wish my sins had not separated us.

JACOB, AFTER ALL HIS MISTAKES, HAD BECOME A GODLY MAN. AND AS HE CONTINUED WALKING THE LORD'S PATH, GOD CONTINUED TO BLESS JACOB AND HIS BLOODLINE THROUGH JOSEPH.

God has promised us a great covenant, Joseph, and you will be the hand that carries it out.

JOSEPH AND HIS DREAMCOAT

Drought and famine are coming. I need to send someone ahead to make arrangements from the inside.

THE STORY OF JOSEPH BEGAN WHEN HE WAS A YOUNG MAN OF SEVENTEEN. HE WAS KIND AND WORKED HARD. JOSEPH'S FATHER AND MOTHER LOVED JOSEPH, BUT SOMETHING WAS NOT RIGHT IN THE FAMILY. JEALOUSY LIVED WITHIN JOSEPH'S STEPBROTHERS.

As the youngest, I always got the hand-me-downs. Now I have a new coat!

IN TIME, HE BECAME THE FAVORITE SON TO JACOB, AND TO SHOW HIS AFFECTION, HE MADE A BEAUTIFUL SLEEVED ROBE OF MANY COLORS FOR JOSEPH TO WEAR.

He is so smug!

Why doesn't father love me most? I am smarter than all of you.

WHEN JOSEPH'S BROTHERS SAW THAT JACOB LOVED JOSEPH MORE, THEY BECAME EVEN MORE JEALOUS. THEY COULD NEVER SAY ANY KIND WORDS ABOUT JOSEPH.

ONE NIGHT, THE LORD GAVE JOSEPH A DREAM. JOSEPH DID NOT KNOW AT THE TIME THAT HIS DREAM WAS TELLING THE FUTURE, SO HE TOLD HIS BROTHERS OF HIS DREAM.

ZZZZZ

JOSEPH'S STEPBROTHERS RESPONDED HARSHLY.

Do you dare think that you will one day be a king?

And we are to bow down to you?

If this is what you think God is telling you, you must be out of your mind.

JACOB SENT ALL HIS SONS, EXCEPT JOSEPH, TO TEND TO THE FLOCKS. THIS WORK WENT ON FOR DAYS, AND THE TIME CAME FOR THE BROTHERS TO HAVE FOOD BROUGHT TO THEM. JACOB GAVE THIS TASK TO JOSEPH. JOSEPH OBEYED HIS FATHER AND SET OUT. IN THE MEANTIME, HIS BROTHERS GRUMBLED ABOUT THEIR WORK.

There they are—they will be so happy to see me!

IT TOOK SOME TIME FOR JOSEPH TO REACH HIS BROTHERS, BUT AFTER A LONG WALK, HE FINALLY SAW THEM IN THE DISTANCE.

AS JOSEPH APPROACHED THEM, THE BROTHERS TALKED ABOUT HOW TO HURT HIM. REUBEN STOOD BACK, NOT FEELING RIGHT ABOUT THE WHOLE THING.

91

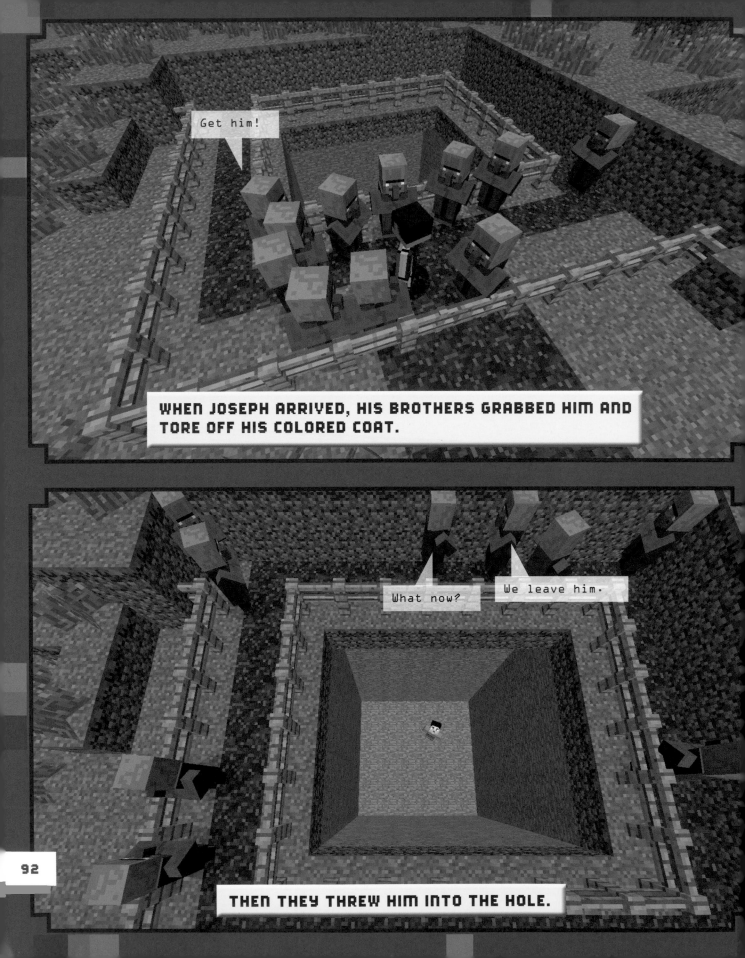

Get him!

WHEN JOSEPH ARRIVED, HIS BROTHERS GRABBED HIM AND
TORE OFF HIS COLORED COAT.

What now?

We leave him.

THEN THEY THREW HIM INTO THE HOLE.

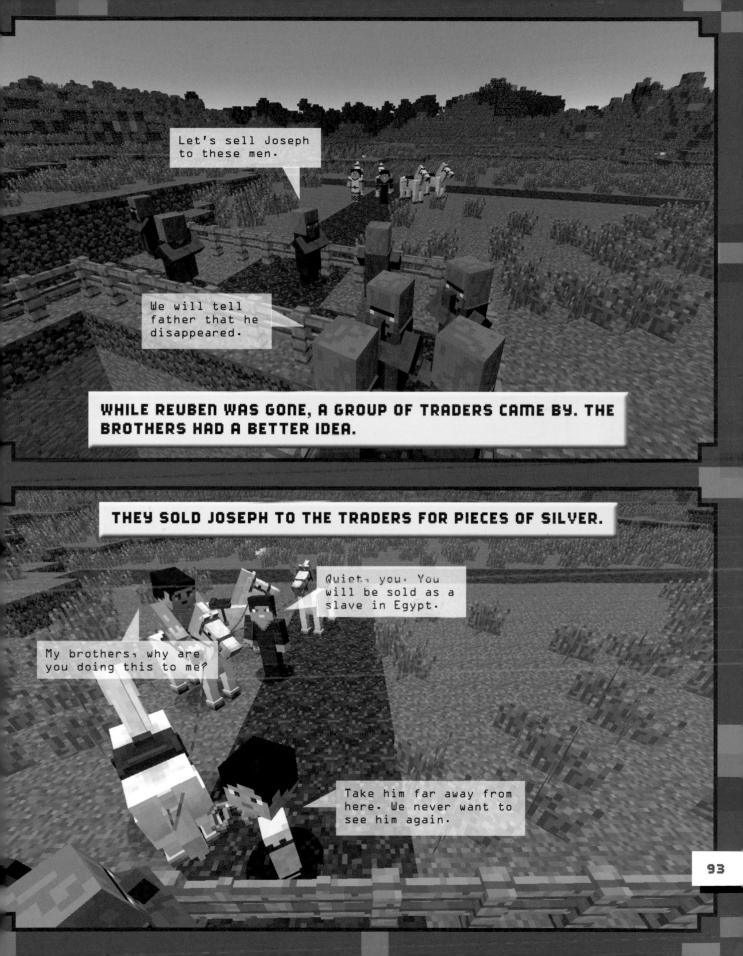

Let's sell Joseph to these men.

We will tell father that he disappeared.

WHILE REUBEN WAS GONE, A GROUP OF TRADERS CAME BY. THE BROTHERS HAD A BETTER IDEA.

THEY SOLD JOSEPH TO THE TRADERS FOR PIECES OF SILVER.

Quiet, you. You will be sold as a slave in Egypt.

My brothers, why are you doing this to me?

Take him far away from here. We never want to see him again.

THE TRADERS SOLD JOSEPH TO AN EGYPTIAN NOBLE NAMED POTIPHAR. HE WAS THE CAPTAIN OF THE PHARAOH'S GUARD AND WAS A VERY IMPORTANT PERSON.

JOSEPH WAS A SLAVE, BUT HE NEVER FORGOT THE VALUES HE WAS TAUGHT. HE WORKED HARD, AND DID NOT HOLD SADNESS IN HIS HEART. IN TIME, POTIPHAR LOVED JOSEPH AND WAS NICE TO HIM. GOD REWARDED POTIPHAR WITH GOOD HARVEST AND MANY RICHES BECAUSE OF THE FAVOR HE SHOWED TOWARD JOSEPH.

I am your servant, as I am God's servant. With such bounty and goodness coming to you, maybe we could talk about my freedom?

I could not have done this without you. I'm sorry, Joseph, I need you by my side.

JOSEPH BECAME AN IMPORTANT MAN IN EGYPT. MANY CAME TO JOSEPH FOR ADVICE AND WISDOM. HOWEVER, IT PAINED JOSEPH THAT HE WAS STILL A SLAVE.

AFTER SOME TIME, JOSEPH COULD SENSE THAT HE WOULD BE FREED, BUT POTIPHAR HAD A VERY SELFISH WIFE. SHE ASKED JOSEPH TO TAKE THE PLACE OF HER HUSBAND. JOSEPH, BEING A MAN OF GOD, REFUSED.

Get back here. I will have you. This I swear!

Get away from me!

JOSEPH WALKED AWAY, BUT POTIPHAR'S WIFE WAS SUCH A ROTTEN WOMAN THAT SHE CAME AFTER JOSEPH AND GRABBED HIM, TAKING PART OF HIS COAT. JOSEPH PULLED AWAY AND RAN OFF, LEAVING HIS COAT BEHIND.

Your slave attacked me! See? Here is part of his coat as evidence!

He did what? How dare he!

POTIPHAR'S WIFE WAS SO ANGRY AT JOSEPH FOR NOT DOING WHAT SHE SAID THAT SHE PLOTTED TO HURT HIM. SHE WENT TO HER HUSBAND, POTIPHAR, AND LIED ABOUT WHAT JOSEPH DID.

Why is this happening to me? What plan does all this serve?

ANGER CLOUDED POTIPHAR'S MIND, AND HE COULD NOT SEE PAST THE LIES. THUS, HE THREW JOSEPH INTO PRISON.

Wait, no...I'm not going to feel sorry for myself. I won't lose faith in God.

JOSEPH MET TWO MEN IN PRISON—PHARAOH'S BUTLER AND BAKER. THE PRISON GUARD ASSIGNED JOSEPH TO TEND TO THESE MEN, AND SO HE CAME TO KNOW THEM.

Joseph, you told me once that you had dreams and that you could interpret them. Please, could you interpret my dream?

It is the Lord that reveals the messages to me.

EACH MAN HAD BEEN HAVING DREAMS THAT TROUBLED HIM.

THE BUTLER TOLD HIS DREAM FIRST: "ON A VINE WERE THREE BRANCHES, AND AS SOON AS IT BUDDED, IT BLOSSOMED AND ITS CLUSTERS RIPENED INTO GRAPES. THEN I HAD PHARAOH'S CUP IN MY HAND, AND I PLUCKED THE GRAPES, CRUSHED THEM INTO PHARAOH'S CUP, AND PUT THE CUP INTO PHARAOH'S HAND."

The three branches represent three days. Within three days, Pharaoh will release you. The cup means you will be back in Pharaoh's favor and serve him personally.

I, too, had a dream, and in my dream there were three baskets on my head. The birds were pecking and eating from the baskets.

THE BAKER STEPPED FORWARD.

Baker, I have interpreted your dream and have some bad news. You will not make it out of prison.

It's good to have you back.

Happy Birthday, my Pharaoh!

THREE DAYS AFTER JOSEPH INTERPRETED THE DREAMS, THE PHARAOH HAD A FEAST IN HONOR OF HIS BIRTHDAY. THE BUTLER WAS LET OUT OF PRISON AND RETURNED TO THE PHARAOH'S SIDE. THE BAKER NEVER SAW HIS FREEDOM AGAIN.

My Pharaoh, I know someone who can help interpret your dream. He is a prisoner.

A prisoner, you say? Very well, I am desperate. I cannot rest until I know what it means. If this man you met in prison can do this, I will give him a great reward.

TWO YEARS PASSED AND JOSEPH REMAINED IN PRISON, UNTIL BY FATE, THE PHARAOH HAD A DREAM. HE CALLED ALL HIS WISEST ADVISORS TO HIM AND ASKED THEM TO INTERPRET THE DREAM . . . BUT NONE COULD.

You, Prisoner! My trusted servant here tells me that you can explain the meaning of dreams.

JOSEPH WAS TAKEN FROM HIS CELL AND BROUGHT BEFORE THE PHARAOH.

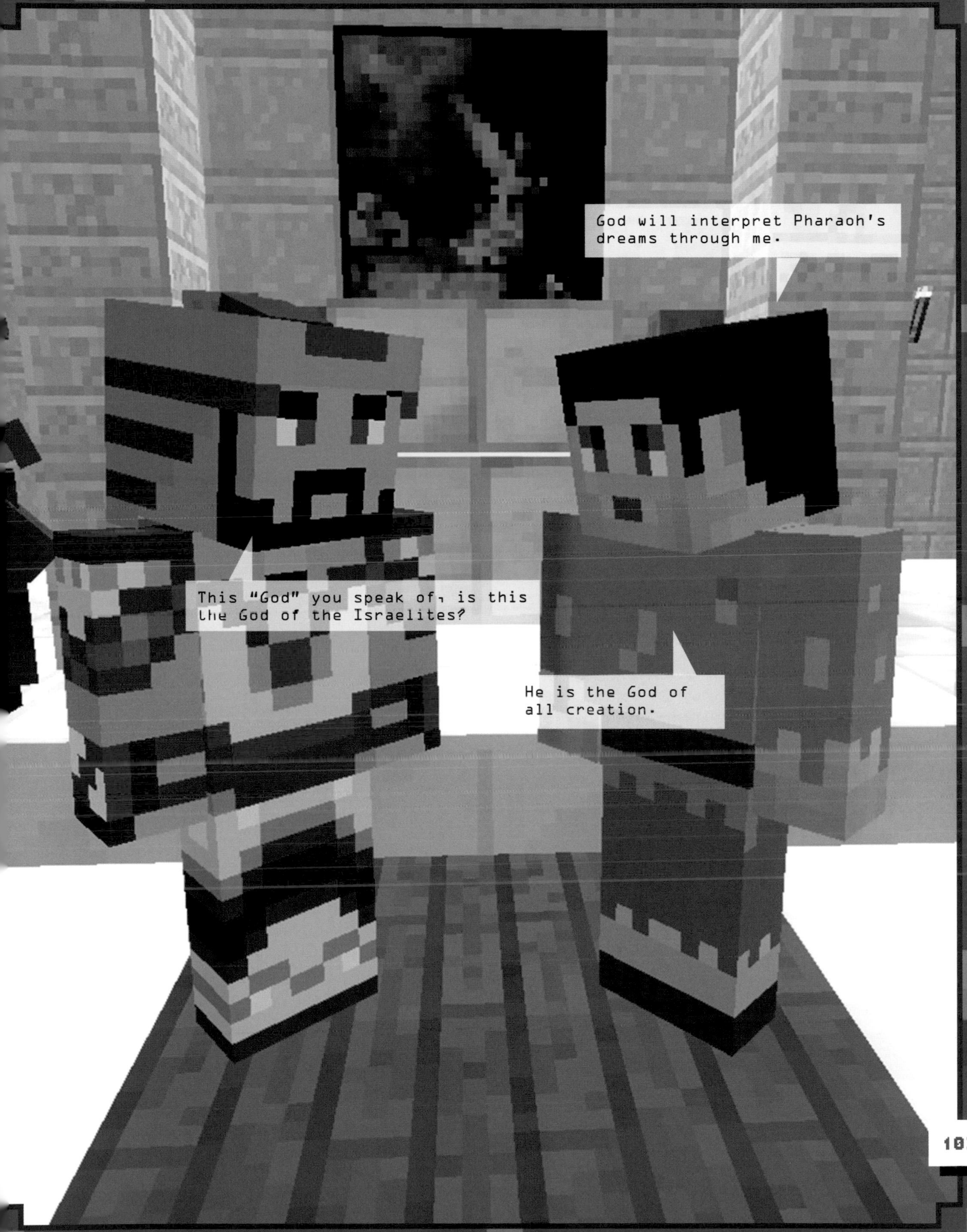
God will interpret Pharaoh's dreams through me.
This "God" you speak of, is this the God of the Israelites?
He is the God of all creation.

THE PHARAOH DID NOT BELIEVE IN THE GOD OF ISRAEL, BUT HE WAS WILLING TO LISTEN. "HERE IS MY DREAM," HE SAID. "I WAS STANDING ON THE BANK OF THE NILE, AND THERE CAME UP FROM THE RIVER SEVEN COWS, FAT AND SLEEK, AND THEY GRAZED ON THE REEDS."

"AFTER THEM, SEVEN OTHER COWS CAME UP THAT WERE POOR, VERY DISEASED AND SICKLY. THEN THE SICKLY COWS ATE UP THE HEALTHY COWS."

God has spoken His plans for you. The seven healthy cows are seven years of good harvest and plenty.

JOSEPH PAUSED.

The seven sickly cows are seven years of famine. When the seven sickly cows eat the healthy cows, that means all the years of plenty will be forgotten, and the famine will ruin the country.

We must do something! I cannot let my people suffer like this.

This is the kind of leadership we need. I hereby appoint Joseph as my hand. He shall be in charge of all matters that concern our food. Only the Pharaoh will have power above him. This I have commanded, so it will be.

JOSEPH SAW THAT THE PHARAOH DID NOT ONLY NEED AN INTERPRETATION OF HIS DREAM, BUT ALSO ADVICE ON WHAT TO DO TO PREVENT THE CALAMITY THAT WAS TO COME.

THE PHARAOH WAS SO IMPRESSED WITH JOSEPH'S WISDOM THAT HE PUT JOSEPH IN CHARGE OF ALL OF EGYPT. JOSEPH SET ABOUT COMPLETING THE TASK OF STORING FOOD FOR THE COMING FAMINE.

Wow, will you look at that! Those Egyptians sure know how to build. It's amazing.

Are we there yet? I have to go to the bathroom.

I've always wanted to see the pyramids.

SEVEN YEARS PASSED, AND JOSEPH COMPLETED HIS TASK. SO MUCH FOOD HAD BEEN STORED THAT WHEN THE FAMINE CAME, NO EGYPTIAN WENT HUNGRY. THE FAMINE DID NOT ONLY STRIKE EGYPT, BUT CAME TO ALL THE LANDS AROUND EGYPT. EVEN THE LANDS OF JACOB, JOSEPH'S FATHER, WERE DESTROYED BY THE FAMINE. JACOB SAW THAT EGYPT HAD FOOD AND SO HE SENT HIS SONS TO EGYPT TO BUY SOME.

Why are you here, strangers?

My lord, we have come to buy food from you, so that we may return home and feed our families.

JOSEPH'S BROTHERS CAME AND BOWED LOW BEFORE HIM. WHEN JOSEPH SAW HIS BROTHERS, HE RECOGNIZED THEM, BUT PRETENDED NOT TO KNOW THEM. THE MEN HAD NO IDEA IT WAS THEIR LONG LOST BROTHER, FOR TIME AND HARDSHIP HAD CHANGED JOSEPH'S LOOKS.

I do not believe you! You are looking to see if we can be conquered. I charge you as spies!

JOSEPH HELD ANGER IN HIS HEART FOR HIS BROTHERS. HE SPOKE HARSHLY TO THEM.

We have come from Canaan. There are twelve of us, all brothers. Our youngest brother is still with our father, and one has disappeared. We just wish for food.

HIS BROTHERS FELL INTO A PANIC. THEY INSISTED THAT THEY WERE NOT SPIES.

One of your brothers disappeared? What happened to him? I'll tell you what, take the food and go home. Return to me with this younger brother so that he may prove your story to be true. Until that time, I will keep one of you here.

Our brother Joseph was the one who disappeared. It breaks our hearts to think about it. We will return with our youngest brother.

JOSEPH DID NOT TRUST HIS BROTHERS. HAD HIS BROTHERS CHANGED, OR WERE THEY STILL AS WICKED AS THEY HAD BEEN? JOSEPH CAME UP WITH A PLAN TO TEST THEM.

Did I not tell you to do poor Joseph no harm? But you would not listen, and now his blood is on our heads, and we must pay.

What are we to do? Father will not let us bring our youngest brother. He won't stand to lose another son.

For when Joseph begged us to stop, we did not listen. That is why these sufferings have come upon us.

109

THE BROTHERS GATHERED TOGETHER. THE KINDEST AND ELDEST OF JOSEPH'S BROTHERS SPOKE.

You came back to these lands as I have ordered you to. You brought your youngest brother as I have commanded. You have done all this and now I find that you have brought a thief with you. Your youngest brother here has been caught stealing from my collection of silver.

No, that is not true!

JACOB LET HIS YOUNGEST SON COME BACK TO EGYPT WITH THE BROTHERS. AT THEIR RETURN, JOSEPH INVITED THEM TO A BANQUET. HE WANTED TO KNOW IF HIS BROTHERS WERE SORRY, SO HE WOULD GIVE THEM ONE MORE TEST. HE ACCUSED THEM OF STEALING.

To punish him for stealing, I will keep your youngest brother, Benjamin, as a slave. That will be his punishment for the thievery!

Please, my lord, take my life instead. Our father lost another son by our hands, and we have been begging for forgiveness. I would give my life if it would undo the wrong I committed against our brother Joseph. Please, do not take Benjamin.

JUDAH, THE OLDEST BROTHER WHO HAD HELD THE MOST JEALOUSY TOWARD JOSEPH, STEPPED FORWARD AND BEGGED HIM.

It sounds like you are truly sorry for what you did.

Yes, truly.

111

WITH THESE WORDS, JOSEPH KNEW THAT HIS BROTHERS HAD TRULY CHANGED AND WERE NOW KIND AND LOVING.

I am your brother Joseph whom you sold into slavery. It was God who sent me ahead of you to save the people of Egypt and Canaan. Go back to my father and give him the good news from his son Joseph. God has made me lord of Egypt. Come, the whole family can stay with me.

JOSEPH COULD NO LONGER CONTROL HIS FEELINGS—ALL THE ANGER WAS GONE NOW, AND ONLY LOVE REMAINED. HE BEGAN TO WEEP.

JACOB AND JOSEPH WERE REUNITED IN EGYPT, AND WITH THE WHOLE
FAMILY, THEY LIVED IN THE LAND OF EGYPT IN PEACE.

THE STORY OF MOSES

Great plan sending them to Egypt!

Thanks! But once again, Gabriel, My Chosen People are under duress.

WHILE IN EGYPT, THE ISRAELITES WERE FRUITFUL AND HAD MANY CHILDREN. THEY INCREASED IN NUMBERS AND BECAME VERY POWERFUL, SO MUCH THAT THE COUNTRY WAS OVERRUN BY THEM.

The Israelites have become too many and too strong. We must be careful to not let them grow powerful in numbers or they will wage war against us.

A NEW KING CAME TO THE THRONE OF EGYPT. HE WAS FEELING OVERWHELMED BY THE ISRAELITES.

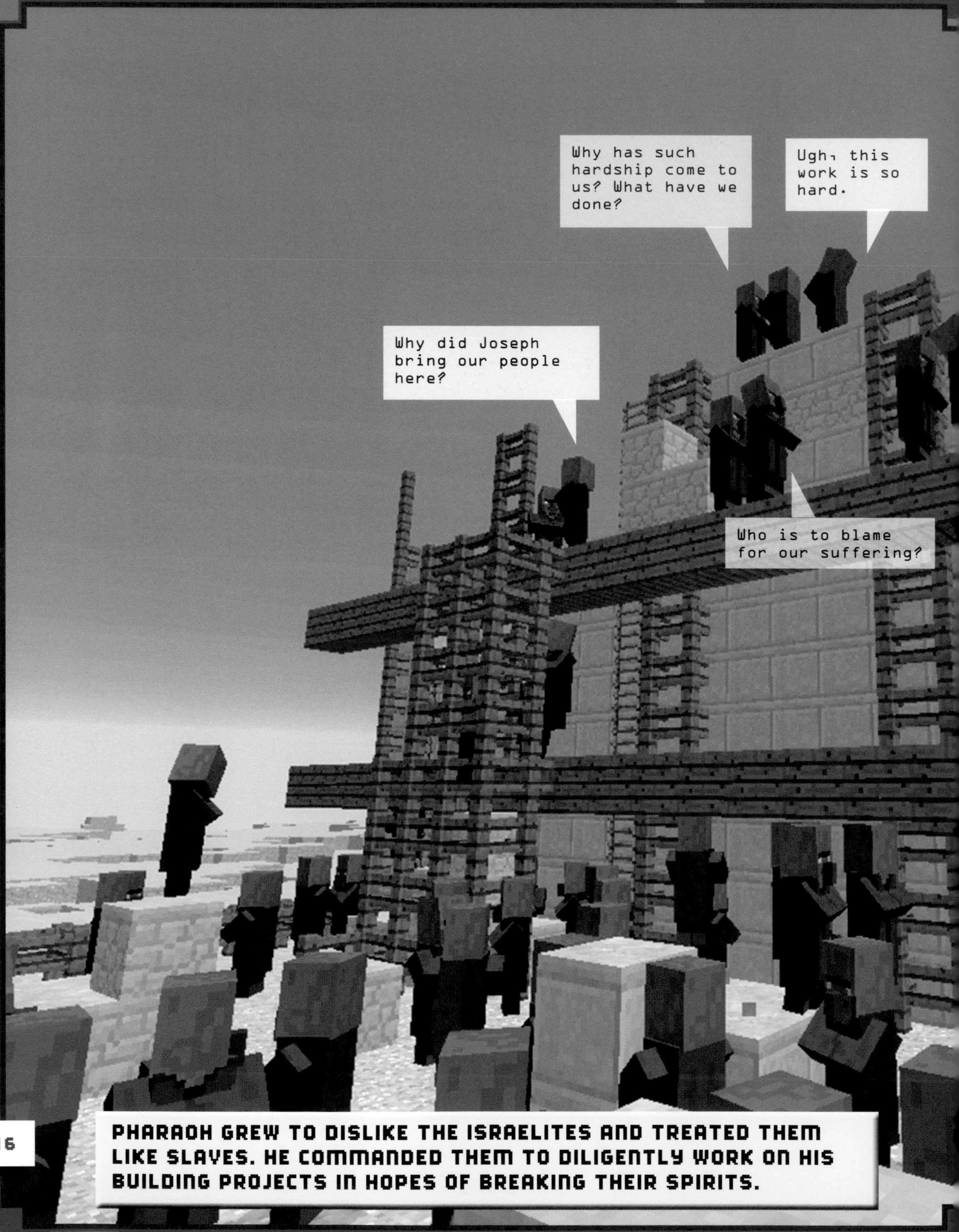
Why has such hardship come to us? What have we done?
Ugh, this work is so hard.
Why did Joseph bring our people here?
Who is to blame for our suffering?
PHARAOH GREW TO DISLIKE THE ISRAELITES AND TREATED THEM LIKE SLAVES. HE COMMANDED THEM TO DILIGENTLY WORK ON HIS BUILDING PROJECTS IN HOPES OF BREAKING THEIR SPIRITS.

THE PHARAOH ANNOUNCED A DECREE THAT ALL NEWBORN ISRAELITE BOYS BE THROWN INTO THE RIVER NILE. PHARAOH WAS DETERMINED TO REDUCE THE NUMBER OF HEBREWS IN HIS LAND.

ONE DAY, A DESCENDANT OF JOSEPH HAD A BABY BOY. THE FATHER AND MOTHER WERE AFRAID OF WHAT WOULD HAPPEN TO THEIR SON, SO THEY DECIDED TO PLACE HIM IN A BASKET THAT WOULD FLOAT DOWN THE RIVER NILE.

AT THAT TIME, THE PHARAOH'S DAUGHTER CAME TO BATHE IN THE RIVER NILE. THE DAUGHTER OF PHARAOH COULD NOT HAVE ANY CHILDREN, AND SHE HAD PRAYED FOR YEARS TO HAVE A BABY.

I will name him Moses!

GOD PROTECTED THE CHILD AS IT WENT DOWN THE RIVER. THE BASKET THEN HIT A FLURRY OF WATER THAT PUSHED THE BASKET TOWARD THE SHORE.

MOSES WAS RAISED BY HIS EGYPTIAN MOTHER, AND LIVED WITH THE PHARAOH'S FAMILY IN THE PALACE. THE PHARAOH TREATED HIM LIKE A SON. WHEN MOSES HAD GROWN INTO A YOUNG MAN, HE WENT OUT AND WITNESSED AN EGYPTIAN OVERSEER STRIKE A HEBREW SLAVE.

Moses, you will be punished by Pharaoh!

Stop! We are all God's creations and need to be kind to one another.

MOSES MOVED IN TO STOP THE OVERSEER, BUT WHILE HE WAS TRYING TO HELP, HE BADLY HURT THE EGYPTIAN.

MOSES WAS AFRAID THE PHARAOH WOULD PUNISH HIM, SO HE RAN AWAY TO THE LAND KNOWN AS MIDIAN TO START A NEW LIFE.

YEARS PASSED, AND THE HEBREWS REMAINED SLAVES. THEY CRIED OUT TO GOD FOR HELP.

MOSES WAS LIVING HAPPILY IN MIDIAN, TENDING TO HIS FLOCKS.

A bush on fire, yet it does not burn up?

Moses, it is I, your Lord. Have no fear.

ONE DAY, MOSES SAW SOMETHING IN THE DISTANCE. HE LEFT HIS FLOCKS AND CLIMBED THE MOUNTAIN TO INVESTIGATE THE STRANGE LIGHT. THE LORD APPEARED TO HIM IN THE FLAME OF A BURNING BUSH.

I hear a voice and see the bush and yet my eyes deceive me. Who called out to me?

MOSES MOVED CLOSER TO THE BUSH.

Moses, I have ultimate power over all the Heavens and Earth. But now I need you, Moses, to fulfill your destiny.

GOD SPOKE AGAIN TO MOSES.

Do not come too close, for I am the Lord, your God. Humble yourself, for you are on holy ground.

MOSES SHOOK AT THE WORDS OF THE LORD AND BOWED LOW.

I have seen the misery of My people in Egypt and I have heard their cries. I will send you to Pharaoh and you shall bring My people out of Egypt.

But who am I that I should go to Pharaoh, and that I should bring the Israelites out of Egypt? I am just a simple man.

I am with you. This shall be the proof that it is I who have sent you: When you have brought the people out of Egypt, you shall all worship the one true God here on this mountain.

If I am to go to the Israelites and tell them that the God of their forefathers has sent me, and they ask me His name, what shall I say?

Tell them you have been sent by Me: I am JEHOVAH!

123

Welcome to Fabulous Egypt!

Home of the Pyramids

Please, walk like an Egyptian

MOSES WOULD DO ALL THAT THE LORD ASKED OF HIM. HE LEFT HIS HOME TO RETURN TO EGYPT.

THE STORY OF THE PLAGUES

Somehow, I have a feeling this isn't going to bode well for the Egyptians.

THE DAY FINALLY CAME WHEN MOSES WENT BEFORE THE PHARAOH. HE STOOD TALL AND BRAVE.

You dare to order me around! You could not be king of Egypt so now you wish to be king of the Israelites? I will never release the people of Israel. They are my slaves.

His people will be free.

Go, Moses, go to your people and be out of my sight.

I fear for you, Pharaoh—you will humble yourself before this is finished.

PHARAOH STOOD FIRM AGAINST GOD'S WILL. SO BEGAN THE EXODUS.

I am Pharaoh of Egypt, a living god on Earth, and I will bow to no one.

Teach these Israelites a lesson—work them harder! I will show them who their master is. Let my tongue be heard by the whip.

As you command, my lord.

PHAROAH'S HEART BECAME HARD WITH WICKEDNESS AND HE SOUGHT TO PUNISH THE INNOCENT. THINGS GOT WORSE FOR THE ISRAELITES.

Do not give them straw to make the bricks, but force them to make the same number of bricks as they have been.

Bricks need straw to be made. How are we to make the same number of bricks without straw to fatten and strengthen them?

THE ISRAELITES PLEADED WITH PHAROAH FOR THE STRAW.

With whips, you will!

129

Lord, why have you brought pain and suffering to your people? Give your people strength!

This is all your fault.

My life is worse now.

THE PEOPLE BLAMED MOSES FOR THEIR TROUBLES. HE PRAYED FOR GUIDANCE.

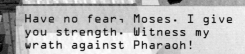

Have no fear, Moses. I give you strength. Witness my wrath against Pharaoh!

WITH THE LORD'S ANSWER, THE TEN PLAGUES OF EGYPT BEGAN.

Let my people go, so sayeth the Lord. If Pharaoh refuses, ten signs will be brought down unto Egypt to show that the one true God rules over all men.

What sign has been given to do this?

MOSES RETURNED TO PHARAOH.

If you wish for a sign, I give this.

MOSES THREW HIS STAFF TO THE GROUND.

Behold the power of the Lord!

Ha, cheap tricks will not move Pharaoh. I am supreme ruler of these lands, and I will not give in to your feeble demands.

131

THE STAFF TURNED INTO A SERPENT.

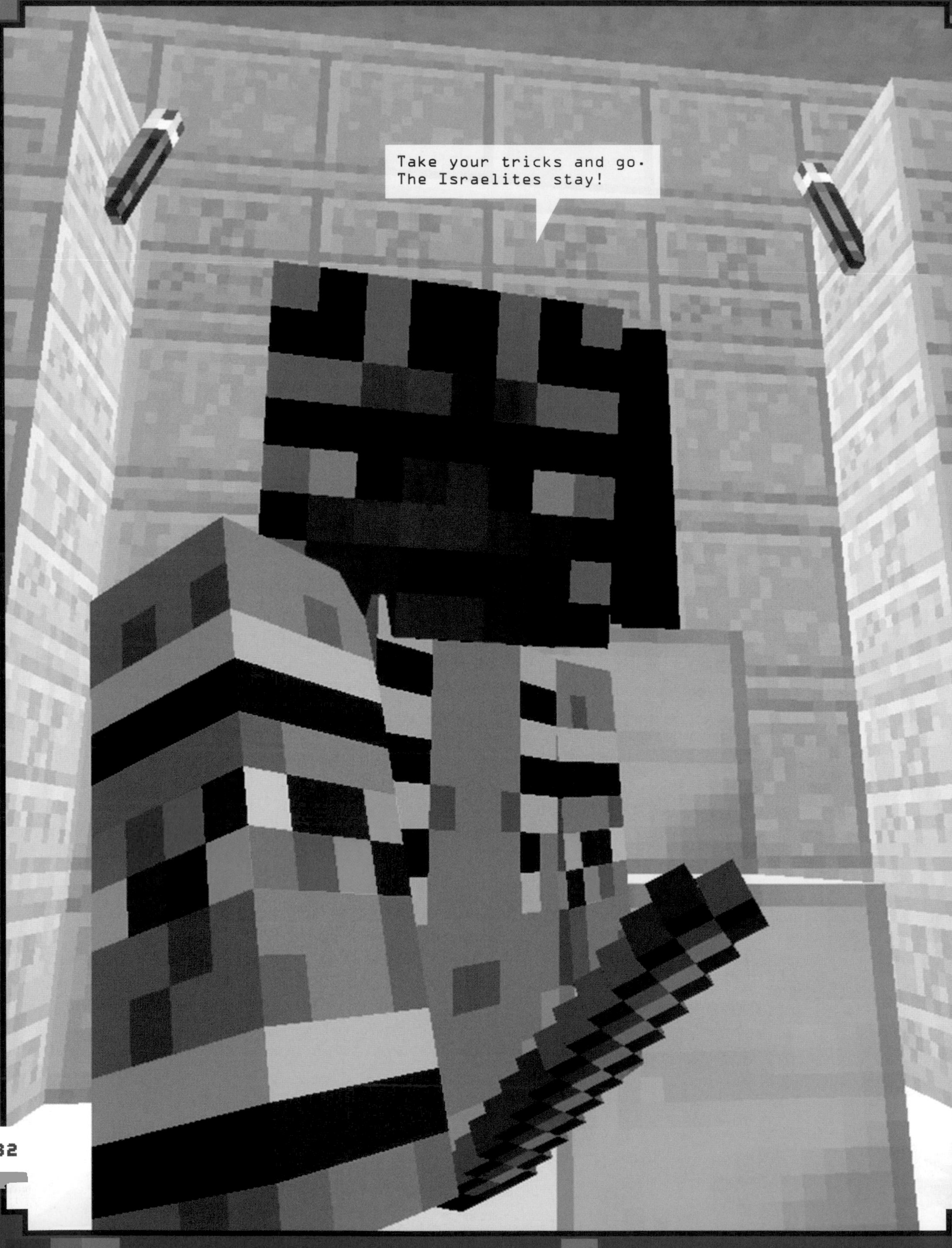
Take your tricks and go. The Israelites stay!

I give you warning again. God will not bend; He has spoken. Will you let my people go?

As I said before, Moses, I will not. I do not fear your god. You still have not shown me any god to fear, as you should fear me.

THE NEXT DAY, MOSES TOLD PHARAOH TO COME TO THE RIVER NILE.

By the power of the Lord, be witness to your stubbornness. The suffering of Egypt will begin and will not stop until you have obeyed the word of the Lord.

MOSES TOUCHED THE WATER WITH HIS STAFF AND THE WATER TURNED TO BLOOD.

You have seen the river turn blood red with God's anger. Now will you set my people free?

I do not know how you did it, Moses, but no, I most certainly will not let your people go!

THE NEXT DAY, MOSES CAME BEFORE THE PHARAOH.

For your stubbornness, you shall see the second plague brought onto your people. May this be the sign you heed and do as the Lord commands.

This cannot be happening. Curse this *God of Moses*. Doesn't he know who he is dealing with? I will never bend to his will!

135

PHARAOH LOOKED OUT THE WINDOW TO FIND ALL OF EGYPT COVERED IN FROGS.

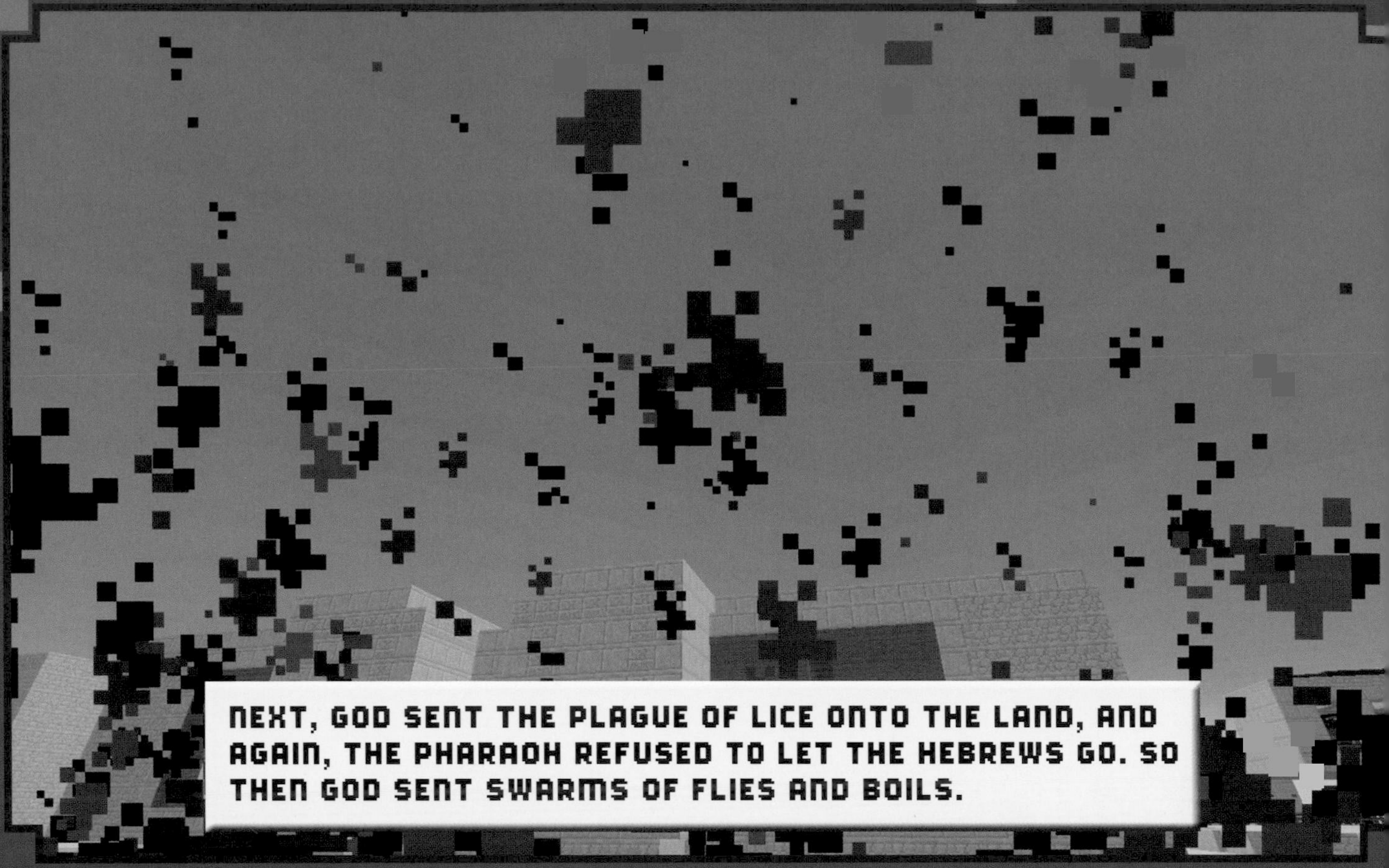
NEXT, GOD SENT THE PLAGUE OF LICE ONTO THE LAND, AND AGAIN, THE PHARAOH REFUSED TO LET THE HEBREWS GO. SO THEN GOD SENT SWARMS OF FLIES AND BOILS.

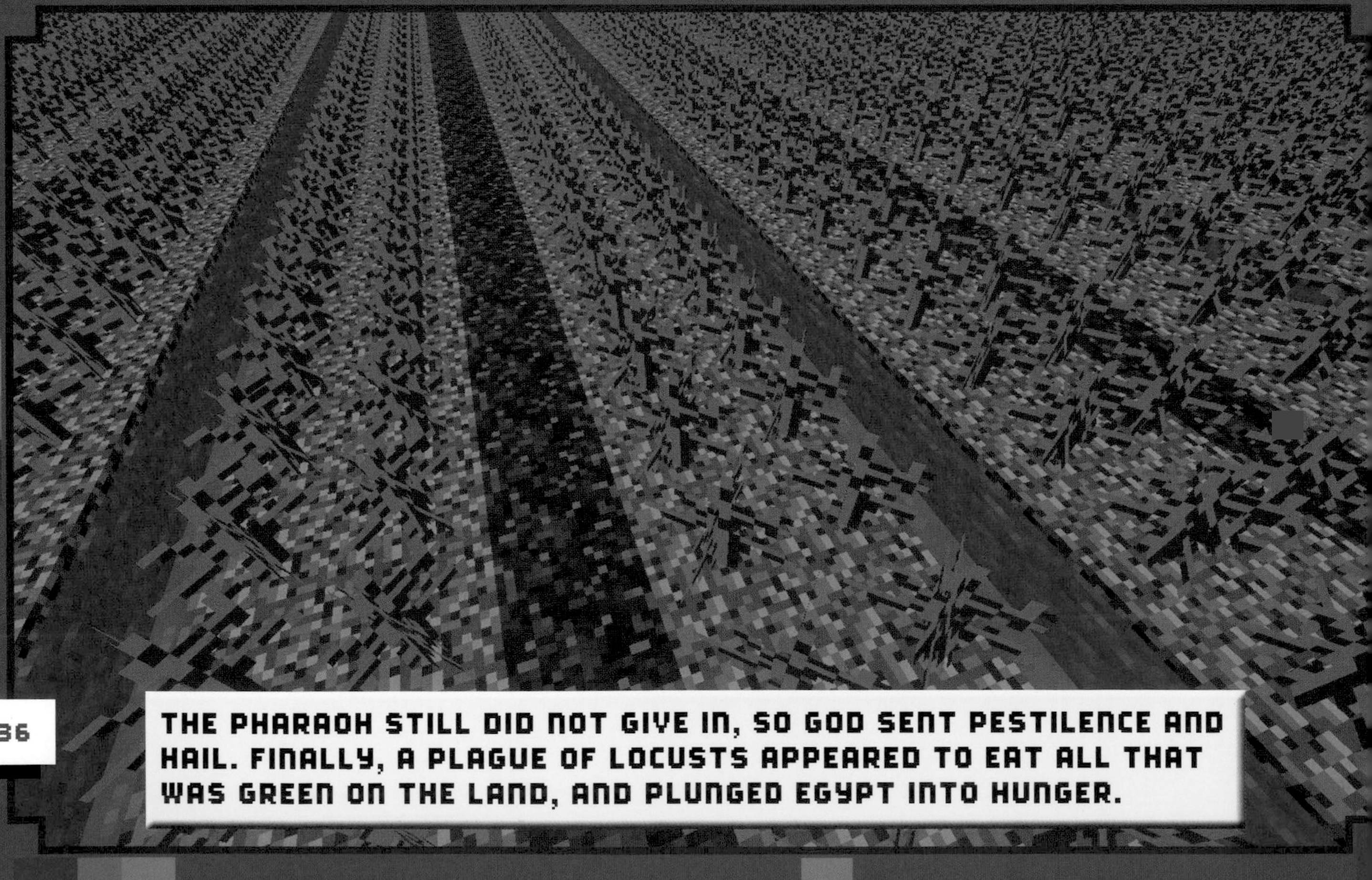
THE PHARAOH STILL DID NOT GIVE IN, SO GOD SENT PESTILENCE AND HAIL. FINALLY, A PLAGUE OF LOCUSTS APPEARED TO EAT ALL THAT WAS GREEN ON THE LAND, AND PLUNGED EGYPT INTO HUNGER.

GOD THEN COVERED THE LAND IN DARKNESS FOR THREE DAYS TO WARN PHARAOH THAT HE MUST RELEASE THE ISRAELITES. BUT PHARAOH STILL WOULD NOT LET THEM GO.

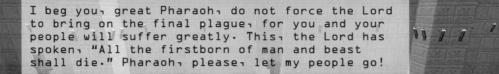

I beg you, great Pharaoh, do not force the Lord to bring on the final plague, for you and your people will suffer greatly. This, the Lord has spoken, "All the firstborn of man and beast shall die." Pharaoh, please, let my people go!

I will never let my slaves go!

HATE AND ANGER SWELLED IN PHARAOH. HE UTTERED THE FATEFUL WORDS THAT DOOMED EGYPT.

SO CAME THE TENTH AND FINAL PLAGUE. GOD TOLD THE ISRAELITES TO PLACE LAMB'S BLOOD ON THEIR DOORPOSTS THAT NIGHT. THIS WOULD SHOW THE ANGEL OF DEATH WHOM TO SPARE.

AS THE ANGEL OF DEATH PASSED OVER EACH HOUSE THAT HELD THE LAMB'S BLOOD, THIS BECAME KNOWN AS THE PASSOVER.

AND THUS THE ANGEL OF DEATH PASSED BY THE DOORS OF ALL THE HEBREWS, WHILE BRINGING A SILENT DOOM TO THE FIRSTBORN OF ALL THE GENTILE FAMILIES OF EGYPT.

AT MIDNIGHT, AS THE TENTH AND FINAL PLAGUE WAS PLAYED OUT, CRIES RANG OUT OVER EGYPT THAT WOULD NEVER BE FORGOTTEN.

MOSES CAME TO THE PHARAOH THE NEXT DAY. HE COULD SEE
THAT PHARAOH HAD A CHANGE OF HEART.

Get out, and take your
people with you.

NOW, FREE FROM THE YOKE OF BONDAGE, THE ISRAELITES SET
OUT WITH MOSES TO THE LAND THAT GOD HAD PROMISED THEM.

PARTING OF THE RED SEA

Sweet, freedom for the Hebrews!

But they're not out of danger yet.

ONCE THE ISRAELITES WERE OUT OF EGYPT, THE PHARAOH, STILL BITTER FROM ALL THE DESTRUCTION BROUGHT ONTO HIS LAND, AMASSED HIS ARMIES, AND ORDERED THEM TO PURSUE THE ISRAELITES.

This God of Israel is a poor General. He has led his people into a trap. Now the only way the Israelites can escape is across the Red Sea. Come, we will take back what is ours.

THE PHARAOH MOVED ACROSS THE DESERT IN PURSUIT OF HIS FORMER SLAVES, AND SOON WAS UPON THEM.

Moses, you have led us to our doom. We are trapped.

The Pharaoh will not show us mercy.

THE ISRAELITES RAN TO THE EDGE OF THE RED SEA. THEY WERE NOW CORNERED, WITH NOWHERE ELSE TO FLEE.

Now that we are on the verge of freedom, do you believe that God would abandon us? Stand firm. The God of Israel will show His power.

MOSES STRETCHED OUT HIS HAND TOWARD THE WATER, FEELING THE PRESENCE OF GOD WITHIN HIM.

Move quickly across the sea. God has saved us!

Look, we are saved.

The Lord has delivered us from bondage.

145

THE PEOPLE WERE ASTONISHED AS THE LORD PARTED THE SEA.

Follow me, we are almost there.

THE PEOPLE OF ISRAEL PASSED BETWEEN THE TWO WALLS OF WATER ONTO DRY LAND.

My Pharaoh, look! The God of Israel has parted the sea. The Hebrews have escaped.

They have not escaped. Order your men to go after them.

THE EGYPTIAN ARMY WENT INTO THE SEA AFTER THE ISRAELITES. MOSES TURNED BACK. HE THEN STRETCHED OUT HIS STAFF AND THE WATERS CLOSED ON PHARAOH'S ARMY.

THE TEN
COMMANDMENTS

It's time I give concrete instructions
for a righteous path in life.

MOSES AND THE PEOPLE OF ISRAEL JOURNEYED TO FIND THEIR
HOMELAND. MOSES BROUGHT THE PEOPLE OF ISRAEL TO THE FOOT
OF MOUNT SINAI. THERE THE LORD WOULD MAKE A COVENANT WITH
THEM.

Moses, join me at the top of the mountain. There I shall give to you the laws to govern men.

MOSES WENT TO MEET WITH GOD. THE MOUNTAIN WAS ABLAZE WITH LIGHT.

THERE AT ITS APEX, MOSES COULD BE SEEN. HE GAVE ONE LAST WAVE TO THE PEOPLE OF ISRAEL BEFORE HE STEPPED OUT OF SIGHT AND WENT TO SPEAK WITH GOD. THE PEOPLE WAVED GOODBYE AND SAID A PRAYER FOR MOSES.

I
You shall have no God before me.

II
You shall not make carved images of Gods.

III
You shall not misuse the Lord's name.

IV
You shall remember the Sabbath Day.

V
You shall honor your mother and father.

VI
You shall not commit murder.

VII
You shall not commit adultery.

VIII
You shall not steal.

IX
You shall not bear false witness.

X
You shall not covet.

Moses, I am the Lord your God who brought you out of Egypt. I give you these laws to live by.

There will be Ten Commandments.

Guide me in Your ways.

151

MOSES FOUND A PLACE THAT WAS QUIET ALONG THE MOUNTAIN CLIFFSIDE. IT WAS THERE GOD SPOKE TO HIM.

I
You shall have
no God before
me.

II
You shall not
make carved
images of Gods.

III
You shall not
misuse the
Lord's name.

IV
You shall
remember the
Sabbath Day.

V
You shall honor
your mother
and father.

I have carved my laws into
the rock. Read them and know
that I am a just and loving
God. Follow my commandments
and you will prosper in life.

VI
You shall not
commit murder.

VII
You shall not
commit
adultery.

VIII
You shall not
steal.

IX
You shall not
bear false
witness.

X
You shall not
covet.

These are My commandments to the world. Now return to My people and teach them My ways.

MOSES THEN LEFT THE MOUNTAIN AND BROUGHT TO THE PEOPLE THE TEN COMMANDMENTS.

THE WALLS OF JERICHO

Nice job on the commandments!

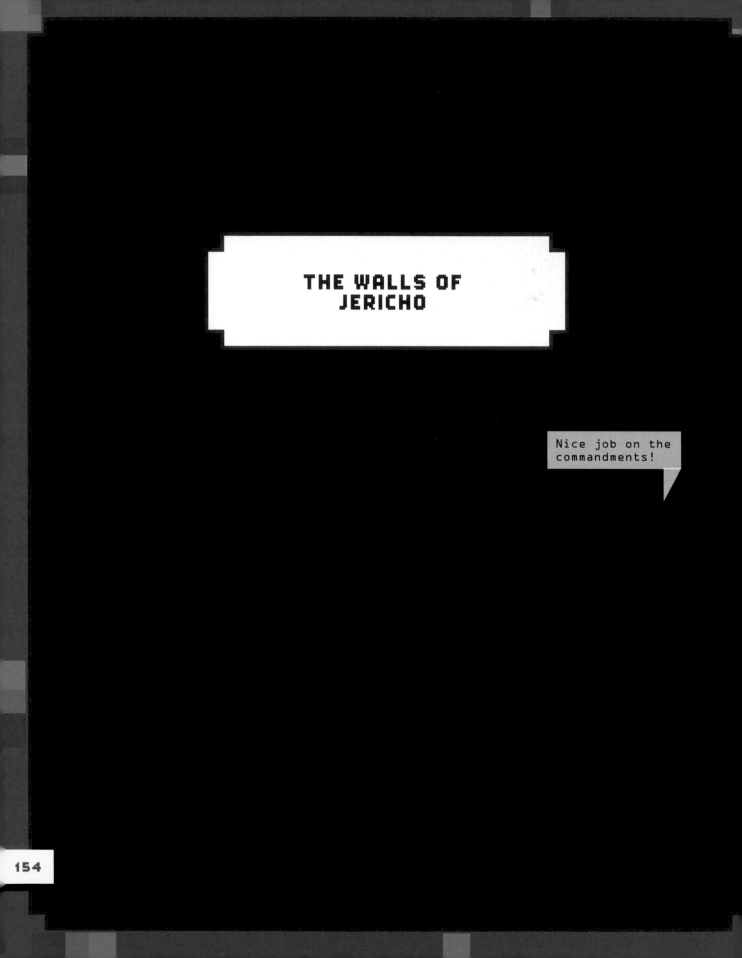

GOD GAVE THE PEOPLE OF ISRAEL TEN COMMANDMENTS TO LIVE BY, BUT IT DID NOT TAKE LONG FOR THEM TO BREAK GOD'S LAWS. SO HE FORBADE ANYONE TO ENTER THE LANDS OF CANAAN. THE ISRAELITES HAD TO WANDER IN THE DESERT FOR FORTY YEARS. GOD THEN MADE IT POSSIBLE FOR THEM TO ENTER CANAAN. ONE LAST MEMBER OF THE OLDER GENERATION REMAINED BEFORE MOSES PASSED AWAY, THUS THE LORD TOLD MOSES TO MAKE JOSHUA LEADER OF THE ISRAELITES.

GOD THEN SPOKE TO JOSHUA AND PROMISED HIM THAT IF THE PEOPLE OF ISRAEL WOULD FOLLOW HIS LAWS, THEN HE WOULD GUARANTEE VICTORY OVER ALL ENEMIES AND PROSPERITY IN THE LAND.

JOSHUA BEGAN TO LEAD THE ISRAELITES INTO THE PROMISED LAND, BUT A GREAT CITY STOOD IN THEIR WAY: THE CITY OF JERICHO. NO ONE COULD EASILY GET PAST THE CITY OF JERICHO INTO THE LANDS OF CANAAN, SO THE ISRAELITES WOULD HAVE TO FIGHT.

Speak to the people and find out what we need to know. Then leave as quietly as you entered.

JOSHUA CALLED ON TWO OF HIS SMARTEST AND BRAVEST CAPTAINS. HE ASKED THEM TO SNEAK INTO JERICHO AND FIND OUT IF THE CITY WAS GOOD OR BAD, AND IF THE CITY WOULD BE AN ENEMY OF ISRAEL.

Spies are somewhere in the city. We will find them and deal with them harshly.

You have done a good job. Now finish it. Go and capture the Israelite spies.

NO SOONER HAD THE TWO SPIES FOR THE ISRAELITES ENTERED JERICHO, THAN THE KING OF JERICHO ORDERED THE MEN CAPTURED.

Will she help protect us?

We will see...

THE TWO SPIES SAW THE SOLDIERS COMING AND RAN TO THE HOUSE OF A WOMAN NAMED RAHAB. SHE HID THE MEN IN THE STRAW THAT COVERED HER ROOF.

Can you help us?

The guards will search, so you must be as quiet as a mouse.

157

Rahab, we have been informed that you are harboring spies.

They just left. If you head out right now, you can catch them.

You better be right, Rahab, or the king will have it in for you.

THE GUARDS POUNDED ON RAHAB'S DOOR.

Thank you for protecting us. I promise you that no harm shall come to you or your family when we take Jericho.

Hang a red cloth out your window and we will instruct our leader that this is the sign of our friend and ally.

I will do so.

ONCE THE GUARDS WERE GONE, RAHAB TOOK THE SPIES TO THE WINDOW THAT LOOKED OUT OVER THE OUTSIDE OF THE CITY.

RAHAB LET THE MEN DOWN A ROPE OUTSIDE THE CITY WALLS.

We have seen the city and it can be taken.

The walls are going to be tough to pass, but we have a friend to help us in our fight.

How will we know who she is?

She will hang a red cloth out her window.

THE SPIES RETURNED TO JOSHUA AND TOLD HIM ABOUT THEIR JOURNEY.

JOSHUA'S ARMY MARCHED TOWARD JERICHO. BETWEEN THE ISRAELITES AND JERICHO WAS THE JORDAN RIVER. THE ISRAELITE ARMY COULD NOT PASS THE RIVER. THE TIME OF THE YEAR HAD MADE IT SWELL AND FLOW OVER ITS BANKS.

GOD TOLD JOSHUA TO HAVE THE PRIESTS CARRY THE ARK OF THE COVENANT TO THE WATER. AS SOON AS THE PRIESTS' FEET TOUCHED THE RIVER, GOD PUSHED ASIDE THE WATERS TO MAKE DRY LAND.

TWELVE STONES WERE PLACED IN THE RIVER BED AND ON THE SHORE IN THE LANDS OF CANAAN.

JOSHUA WAS MET BY AN ANGEL OF THE LORD. THE ANGEL SAID THAT HE WAS SENT BY GOD TO TELL JOSHUA HOW TO DEFEAT THE POWERFUL CITY OF JERICHO.

Take the priest and the Ark ahead of the army. March around the city. For six days, you are to do this without attacking. On the seventh day, you are to march around the city seven times. On the final time, you are to blow your rams' horns and cry out. At that time, you shall have your victory.

THE ANGEL INSTRUCTED JOSHUA THAT THE LORD WOULD BRING DOWN THE WALLS OF JERICHO, THAT IT WAS THE FAITH OF THE PEOPLE THAT WAS NEEDED AND VICTORY WOULD BE THEIRS.

ON THE SEVENTH TIME AROUND THE CITY, THE PRIESTS BLEW THEIR HORNS AND THE ARMY SHOUTED WITH ALL THEIR MIGHT. A RUMBLE WAS HEARD AND CRACKS FORMED IN THE WALLS. AS THE NOISE CONTINUED, THE WALLS OF JERICHO CAME TUMBLING DOWN. THE CITY FELL TO JOSHUA.

THE STORY OF SAMSON

AGAIN, THE ISRAELITES DID EVIL IN THE EYES OF THE LORD, SO HE PUT THEM UNDER THE CONTROL OF THE PHILISTINES.

The time has come for the people of God to be freed. You will have a child that will be judge over all of Israel.

AN ANGEL OF THE LORD APPEARED TO AN ISRAELITE WOMAN.

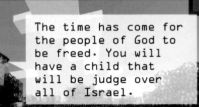

His hair is never to be cut, for it is the Lord's commandment. He will be given great strength as long as he does not stray from the path of God.

THAT EVENING THE WOMAN AND HER HUSBAND PREPARED A BURNT OFFERING FOR THE BLESSING THE LORD WOULD GIVE THEM.

But that is ours.

It's mine now. I'm stronger than you, so I can take it.

TO THE ISRAELITE COUPLE, A SON WAS BORN, BUT HE GREW INTO A MAN THAT HAD TROUBLE OBEYING GOD. WITH HIS GREAT STRENGTH CAME TREMENDOUS PRIDE, AND IT WOULD LEAD TO HIS DOWNFALL.

I found the woman I want to marry

WHEN SAMSON BECAME A MAN, HE WENT TO TOWN AND SAW A BEAUTIFUL PHILISTINE WOMAN. HE RETURNED HOME TO TELL HIS PARENTS OF HIS PLAN TO MARRY HER.

Must you marry an evil Philistine woman?

But son, she is a Philistine! Is there not one woman from God's people that you like?

Give me what I want!

SAMSON WENT OUT TO VISIT HIS FUTURE BRIDE, BUT HE WAS ATTACKED BY A LION ON THE ROAD.

THE POWERFUL SPIRIT OF THE LORD CAME OVER HIM.

WITH HIS BARE HANDS, SAMSON GRABBED HOLD OF THE LION AND WRESTLED THE BEAST WITH ALL HIS MIGHT.

I have become unstoppable!

SAMSON FOUGHT THE MASSIVE CREATURE.

HE SLAMMED THE BEAST SO HARD TO THE GROUND AGAIN, ITS REAR END STOOD ERECT.

WHEN SAMSON TRAVELED THE ROAD AGAIN, HE FOUND THE LION COVERED IN BEES.

The bees have made honey. This is my reward from God!

Hmm, something sweet from a beast?

SAMSON SCOOPED SOME HONEY UP.

THAT NIGHT, SAMSON THREW A FEAST FOR HIS BRIDE.

Let me tell you a riddle.

SAMSON LOVED TO PROVE HIS SUPERIORITY OVER OTHERS, SO HE PRESENTED THE MEN AT THE PARTY WITH A MIND-BENDING QUESTION.

If you can give me the answer, I will give you thirty garments.

We accept.

Complete this riddle: Out of the eater, something to eat; out of the strong, something sweet.

167

What are we to do? I am not giving anything to that Israelite.

I have an idea.

Did you invite us here just so your husband can swindle away our property? Get us the answer or else!

I'll try.

SHE CRIED THE WHOLE SEVEN DAYS OF THE FEAST. ON THE FINAL DAY, SAMSON BROKE DOWN AND TOLD HER THE ANSWER TO THE RIDDLE.

If you love me, you'll give me the answer to your riddle.

Fine, I will tell you. The answer is: "A lion and honey."

168

SAMSON'S WIFE CRIED TO HER HUSBAND.

SAMSON'S WIFE LEFT HIM AND WENT BACK TO THE MEN.

I have the answer.

Nice!

You have done well. No harm will come to you.

THE MEN TOOK THE ANSWER BACK TO SAMSON.

We have the answer.

What is sweeter than honey? What is stronger than a lion?

If you had not gone to my wife, you would not have the answer! You have betrayed me.

169

SAMSON SPOKE TO THEM IN GREAT ANGER.

ENRAGED, HE WENT DOWN TO ASHKELON TO CLAIM HIS "PRIZES."

IN NO TIME FLAT, SAMSON STRUCK DOWN THIRTY PHILISTINES AND THEN TOOK THEIR GARMENTS.

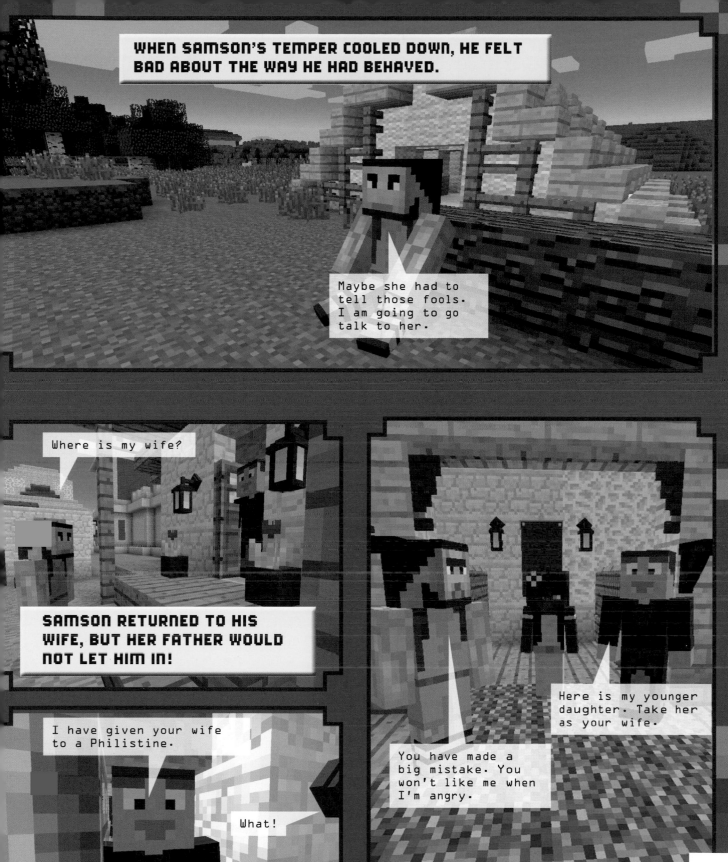

WHEN SAMSON'S TEMPER COOLED DOWN, HE FELT BAD ABOUT THE WAY HE HAD BEHAVED.

Maybe she had to tell those fools. I am going to go talk to her.

Where is my wife?

SAMSON RETURNED TO HIS WIFE, BUT HER FATHER WOULD NOT LET HIM IN!

I have given your wife to a Philistine.

What!

Here is my younger daughter. Take her as your wife.

You have made a big mistake. You won't like me when I'm angry.

171

SAMSON STORMED AWAY.

SAMSON WAS HURT AND HE ACTED WITHOUT THOUGHT OF HOW A GODLY MAN SHOULD ACT.

This time, I have a right to get even with the Philistines.

HE CAUGHT THREE HUNDRED FOXES, ATTACHED TORCHES TO THEIR TAILS, AND SET THEM AMONG THE WHEAT FIELDS.

SOON, THE PHILISTINES WENT AFTER SAMSON.

172

ONCE AGAIN, SAMSON AND THE PHILISTINES FOUGHT A GRUELING BATTLE.

AND ONCE AGAIN, SAMSON WAS VICTORIOUS.

I will wait until people forget what I have done.

AFTER THE FIGHT, SAMSON WENT DOWN TO ETAM AND HID IN A CAVE.

BUT THE PHILISTINES DID NOT FORGET OR FORGIVE. THEY GATHERED AN ARMY AND MADE CAMP IN JUDAH.

Why have you come?

Give us Samson.

We have come to turn you over to the Philistines.

Very well. I will not resist you.

MEN FROM JUDAH WENT DOWN TO THE CAVE.

My lord, I humble myself before you.

SO THEY BOUND HIM WITH ROPE AND LED SAMSON OUT TO THE PHILISTINES.

THE PHILISTINES SAW SAMSON AND SHOUTED WITH RAGE. A MOB RUSHED AND ATTACKED HIM.

My people are very angry.

May God help me.

THE LORD HEARD SAMSON AND HIS SPIRIT CAME POWERFULLY UPON HIM. HE BROKE FREE OF THE ROPES AND PICKED UP THE JAWBONE OF A DONKEY.

SAMSON FOUGHT FURIOUSLY AGAINST THE ONSLAUGHT OF MEN AND METAL.

ONE AFTER ANOTHER, THE PHILISTINES FELL TO SAMSON.

HIS VICTORY WAS SO GREAT THAT THE PHILISTINES FLED HIS PATH.

With a donkey's bone, I have made donkeys of them.

Lord, please give me water to quench my thirst.

THE LORD OPENED A HOLLOW PLACE AND A SPRING CAME UP. SAMSON'S STRENGTH WAS RENEWED.

SAMSON AND DELILAH

I do not fear any Philistines, because I am greater than all people.

I just saw Samson.

Good. Once he's inside, close the gate. We will trap him.

178

We will attack him in the morning. Gather all the men you can.

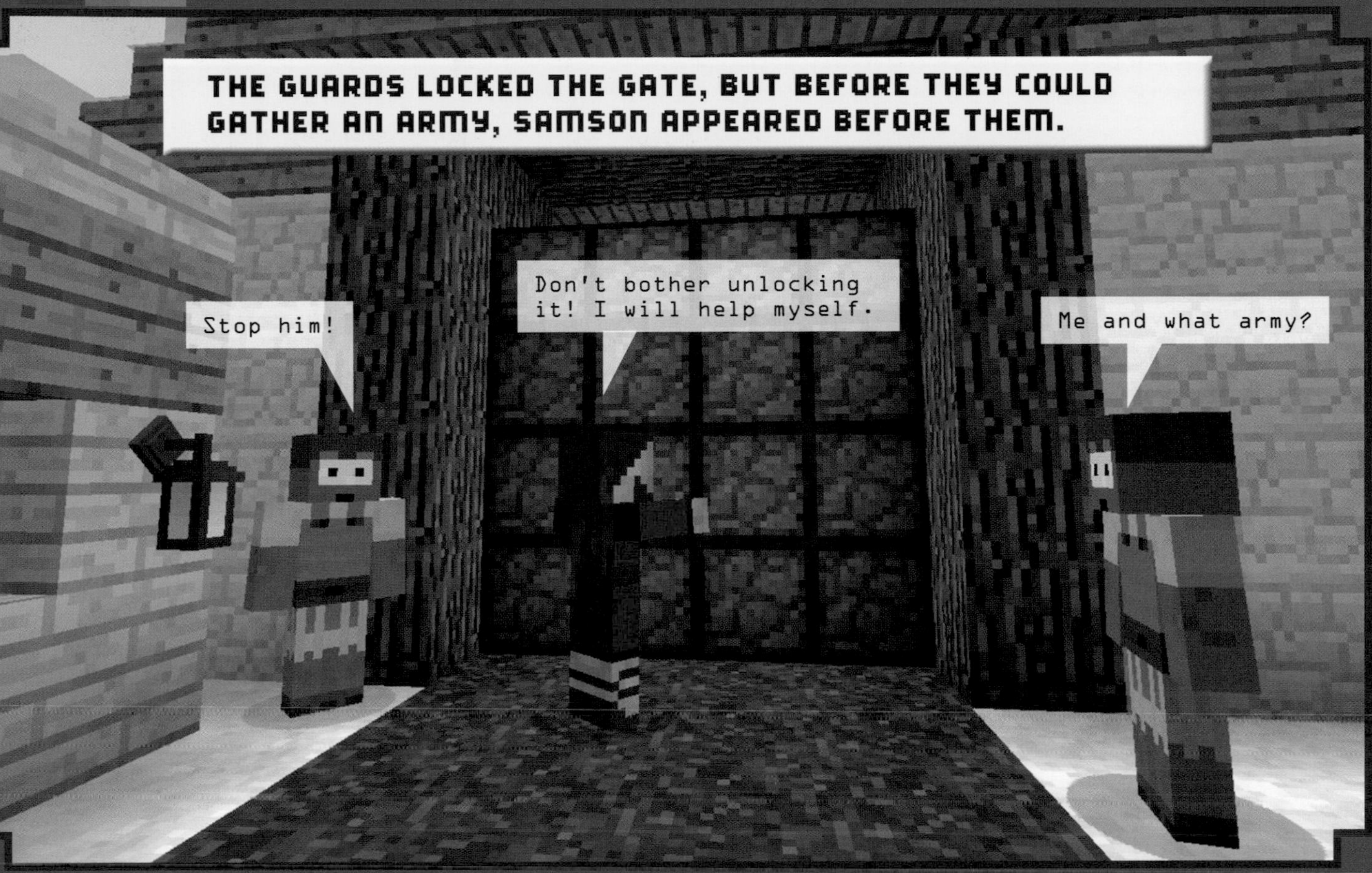
THE GUARDS LOCKED THE GATE, BUT BEFORE THEY COULD GATHER AN ARMY, SAMSON APPEARED BEFORE THEM.
Stop him!
Don't bother unlocking it! I will help myself.
Me and what army?

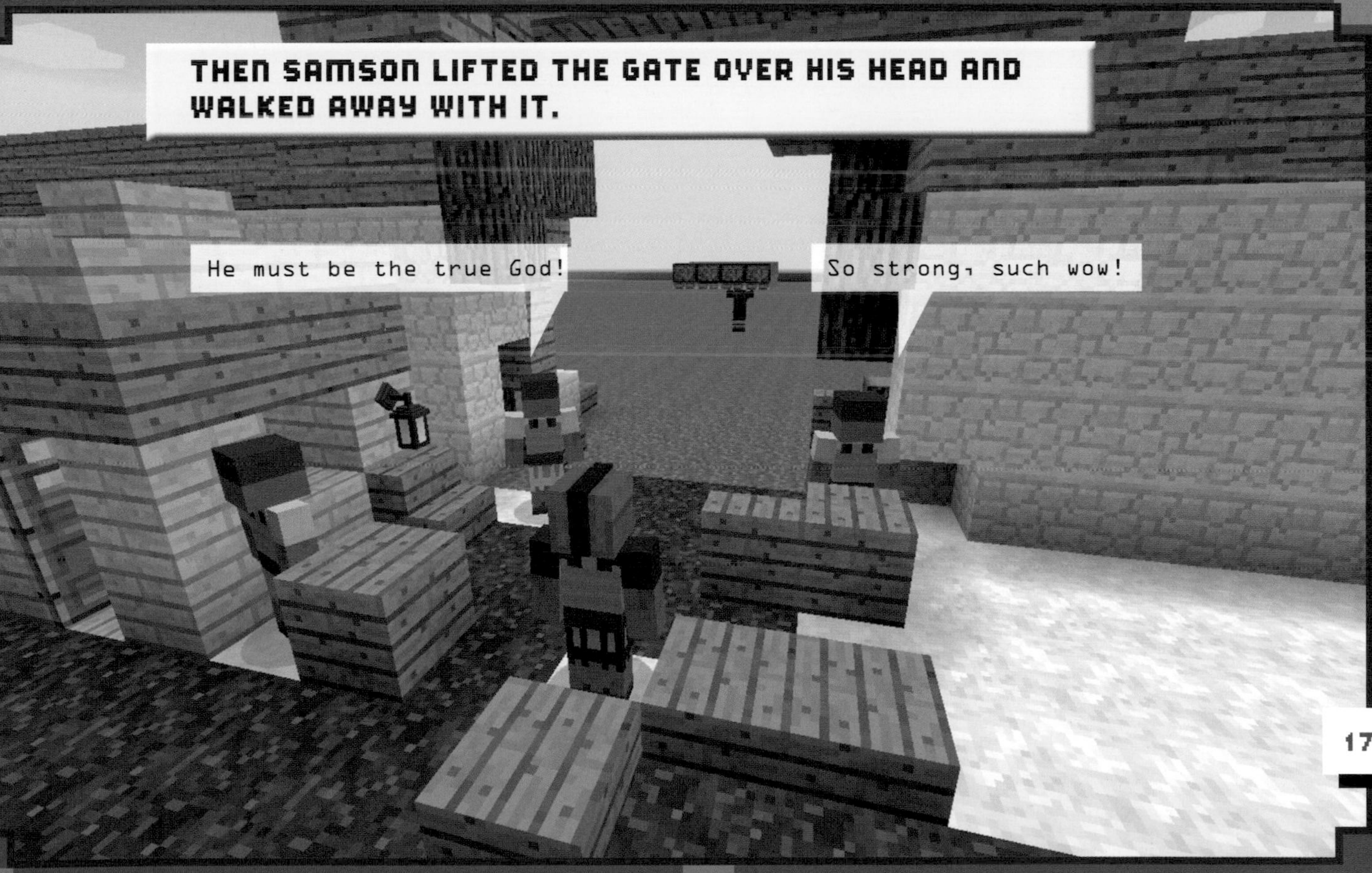
THEN SAMSON LIFTED THE GATE OVER HIS HEAD AND WALKED AWAY WITH IT.
He must be the true God!
So strong, such wow!

Your hair is so beautiful.

As is yours.

SOMETIME LATER, SAMSON FELL IN LOVE WITH A WOMAN NAMED DELILAH.

THE RULERS OF THE PHILISTINES MET AS A COUNCIL TO DISCUSS HOW TO DEAL WITH SAMSON.

There must be a way.

He is unstoppable.

Samson must have a weakness. We just need to find out what it is.

How do we do that?

We will pay a woman to find out his weakness.

I know the exact person, Delilah. She can be bought, for her first love is money.

180

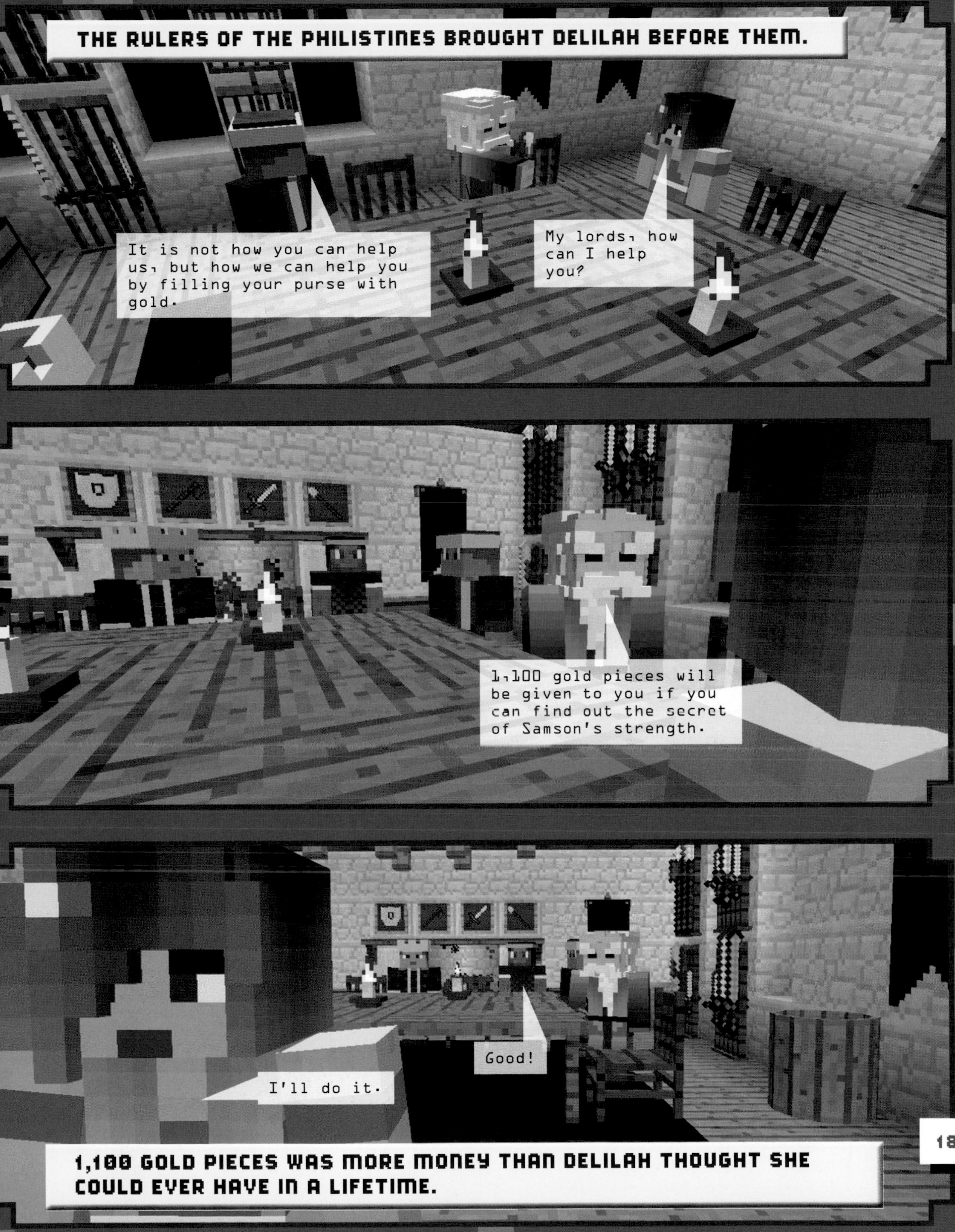
THE RULERS OF THE PHILISTINES BROUGHT DELILAH BEFORE THEM.
My lords, how can I help you?
It is not how you can help us, but how we can help you by filling your purse with gold.
1,100 gold pieces will be given to you if you can find out the secret of Samson's strength.
I'll do it.
Good!
1,100 GOLD PIECES WAS MORE MONEY THAN DELILAH THOUGHT SHE COULD EVER HAVE IN A LIFETIME.

Samson, my dear, tell me the secret of your strength.

If anyone ties me with seven fresh bowstrings, I lose my strength.

WHILE SAMSON SLEPT, DELILAH TIED HIM UP.

SAMSON AWOKE, THEN JUMPED UP AND SNAPPED THE ROPES.

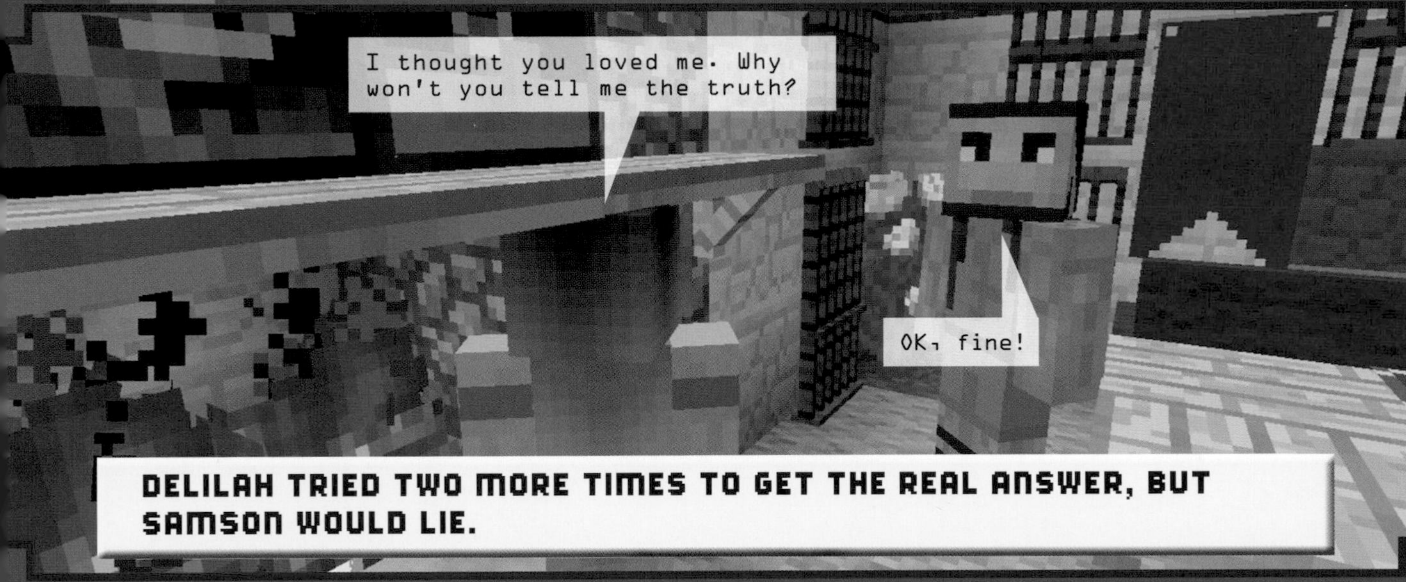
I thought you loved me. Why won't you tell me the truth?
OK, fine!
DELILAH TRIED TWO MORE TIMES TO GET THE REAL ANSWER, BUT SAMSON WOULD LIE.

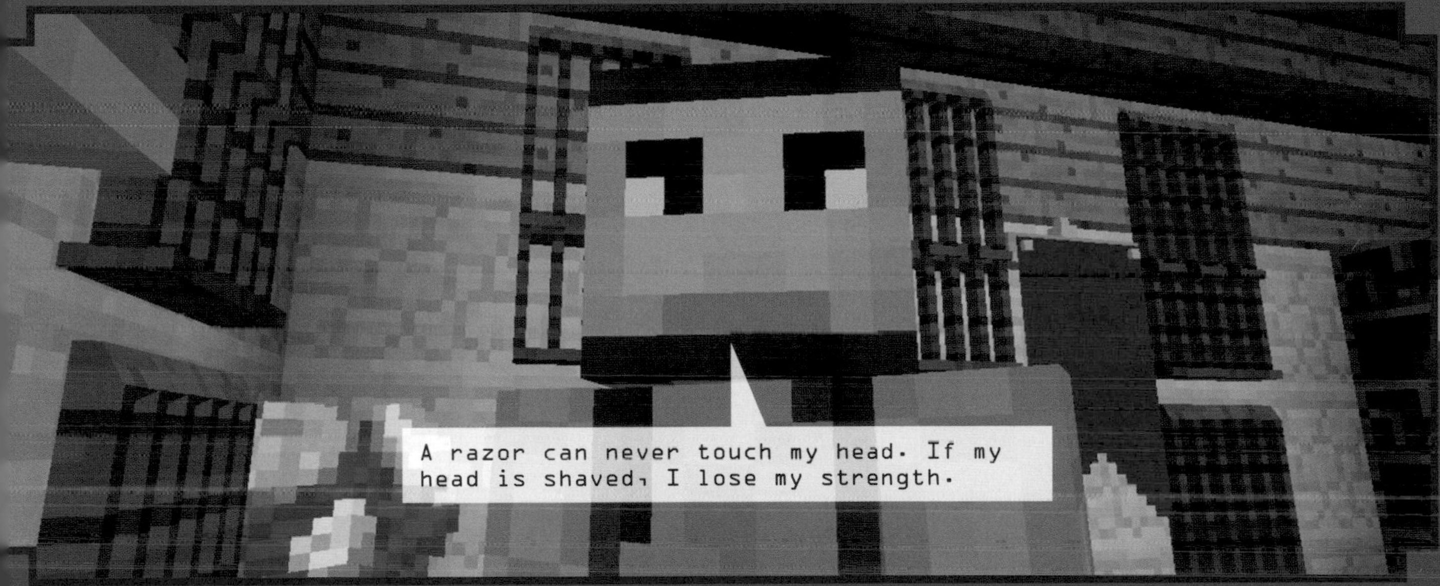
A razor can never touch my head. If my head is shaved, I lose my strength.

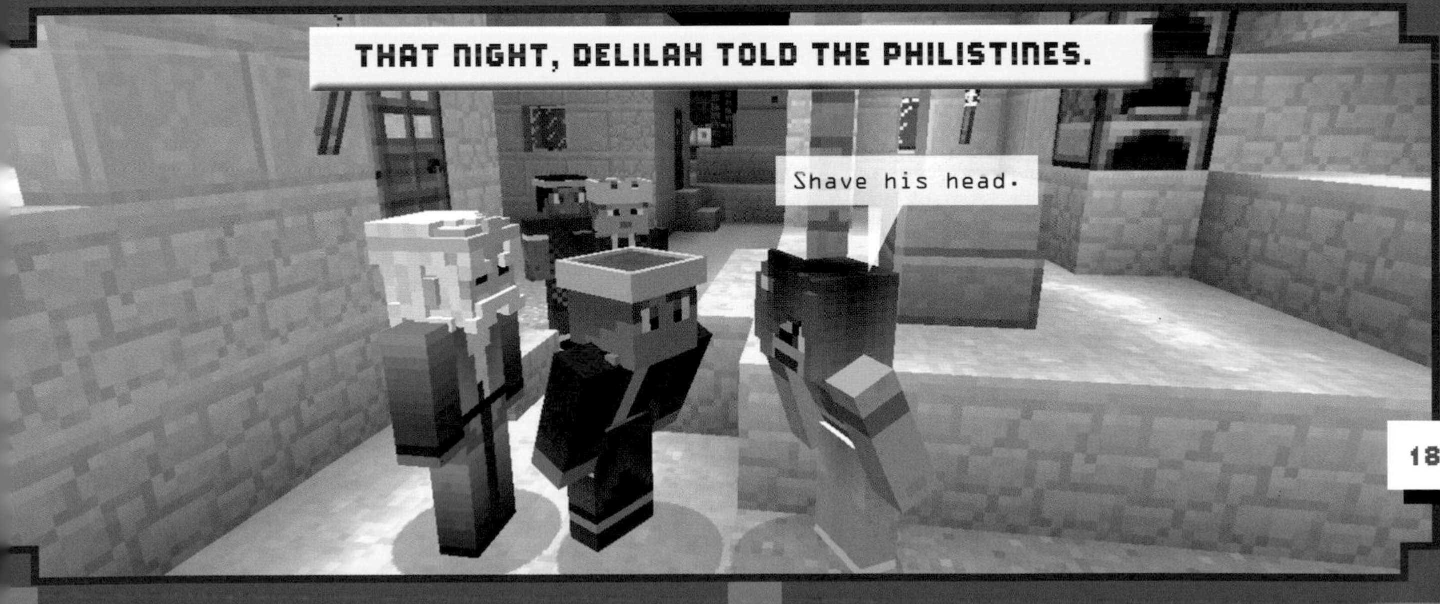
THAT NIGHT, DELILAH TOLD THE PHILISTINES.
Shave his head.

He is in there.

WHILE SAMSON SLEPT, THEY CUT HIS HAIR.

184

We have you now.

WHEN HE AWOKE, THE PHILISTINES SEIZED HIM.
SAMSON WAS AS WEAK AS A BABY.

SAMSON WAS ESCORTED TO
PRISON, WHERE HE AWAITED
HIS PUNISHMENT.

SOON, THEY SENT HIM TO THE
PITS TO GRIND GRAIN, AND TO
THE MINES TO GATHER PRECIOUS
MATERIALS, AND THEN LATER,
THEY REMOVED HIS EYESIGHT.

DELILAH RETURNED TO THE
LEADERS TO RECEIVE HER
REWARD.

Here is your money.

I'm rich!

AS SAMSON TOILED THROUGH HIS IMPRISONMENT, THE HAIR ON HIS HEAD BEGAN TO GROW.

IN THE TEMPLE, THE PHILISTINES GATHERED FOR A GREAT CELEBRATION.

WHILE THE CROWD WAS IN HIGH SPIRITS, THEY SHOUTED FOR SAMSON.

Bring out Samson!

SAMSON WAS BROUGHT BEFORE THE CROWD.

Welcome, Samson, perhaps you can perform a few tricks for our entertainment.

Behold the once mighty Samson!

Boy, put me where I can feel the pillars that hold up the temple.

They are here.

SINCE HE WAS UNABLE TO SEE, SAMSON RELIED UPON A YOUNG BOY TO HELP HIM AROUND THE STAGE.

Now, my child, RUN!

187

SAMSON REACHED FOR THE PILLARS.

Oh Lord, I have disobeyed you far
too long. My time has come—let me
die with the Philistines.

THEN THE STRENGTH OF THE LORD CAME OVER SAMSON AND HE PUSHED AGAINST THE PILLARS WITH ALL HIS MIGHT. THE TEMPLE CAME DOWN ON SAMSON AND ALL THE PHILISTINES.

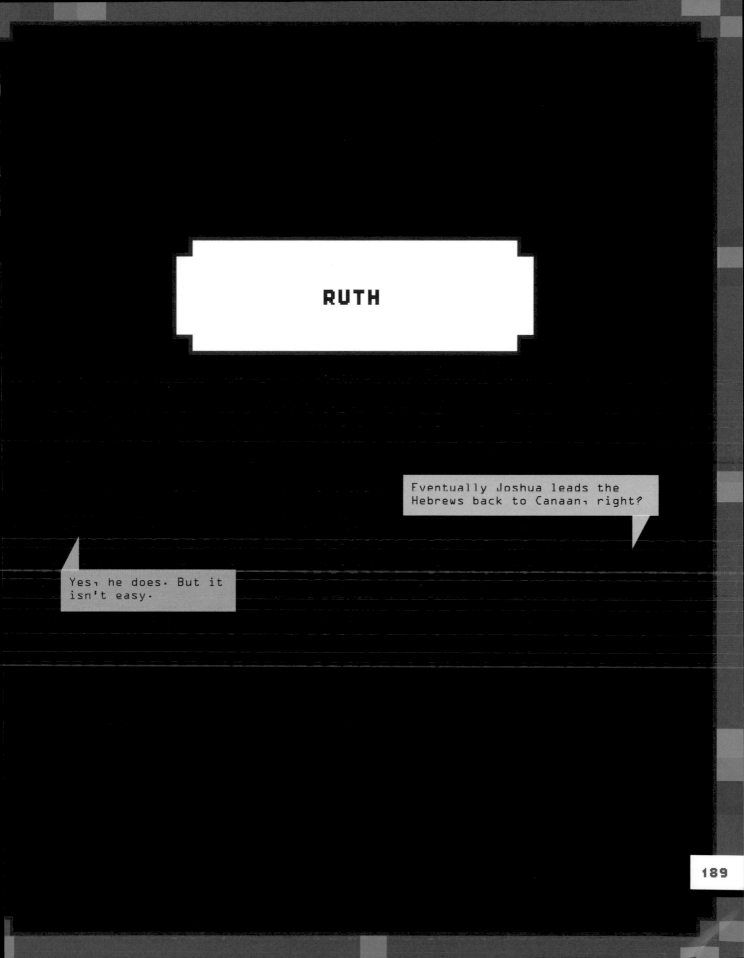

RUTH

Eventually Joshua leads the Hebrews back to Canaan, right?

Yes, he does. But it isn't easy.

WE BEGIN OUR STORY OF RUTH AND THE BLOODLINE OF JESUS LONG AFTER THE GREAT LEADER JOSHUA DIED. IN THIS TIME, JUDGES RULED OVER THE ISRAELITES. THERE WAS A FAMINE IN THE LANDS OF CANAAN. MANY PEOPLE FLED THEIR HOMES TO TRAVEL TO OTHER LANDS.

Husband, I am fearful of the Moabites. They are not like us and practice against God's ways. I am afraid that our family will begin to worship idols or marry Moabite women.

Our new life will be with God, but it must be in the lands of Moab for now. Our sons will have to marry and they will be Moabite women. Have no fear, you have raised them well.

AN ISRAELITE NAMED ELIMELECH LEFT BETHLEHEM TO LIVE WITH THE MOABITES. HE WANTED TO ESCAPE FAMINE. THE MOABITES LIVED TO THE EAST OF JUDAH AND THE DEAD SEA. THERE, THE LANDS STILL BROUGHT FORTH FOOD FOR THE PEOPLE.

Father, what are we to do if we are asked to worship idols?

We must politely say "No." Remember the first commandment, "You shall not have any other gods before me."

191

IN TIME, ELIMELECH'S SONS MARRIED MOABITE WOMEN. ONE WAS NAMED ORPAH AND THE OTHER, RUTH.

SHORTLY AFTER THE MARRIAGES, ELIMELECH AND HIS TWO SONS DIED.

My daughters, please return to your fathers and start your lives over. You are young and can marry again.

How will you care for yourself?

THE FAMINE THAT PLAGUED THE LANDS OF JUDAH HAD PASSED. ELIMELECH'S WIFE, NAOMI, DECIDED TO RETURN TO HER HOMELAND OF BETHLEHEM. THERE, SHE HOPED TO FIND RELATIVES THAT WOULD CARE FOR HER.

OK, see ya around.

ORPAH LEFT NAOMI.

RUTH REFUSED TO LEAVE NAOMI'S SIDE, FOR SHE NOW BELIEVED IN THE ONE TRUE GOD.

I will miss my adopted home, but I look forward to returning to Bethlehem.

SO NAOMI AND RUTH LEFT MOAB AND RETURNED TO BETHLEHEM.

Don't despair, Mother. With a little bit of work we can make it a home again.

Look at this mess! The birds and mice have had their fill of this house.

Look at the house now. With just a few decorations, it will be better than our home in Moab.

We should think about finding food.

195

NAOMI HAD A KINSMAN, BOAZ, WHO WAS VERY RICH. HE OWNED A GREAT FARM THAT COULD FEED MANY PEOPLE.

We have a custom in our land: A woman without a family can go to any person's farm and pick up what is left behind. So, if the farmers leave some food behind, we can have it.

Mother, how can we get food from your relative, Boaz?

RUTH LEFT AND HEADED OVER TO BOAZ'S FARM.

AT BOAZ'S FARM, RUTH BEGAN FOLLOWING THE WORKERS AS THEY CUT DOWN THE WHEAT. AS THEY LEFT PIECES, SHE WOULD GATHER THEM UP. FINALLY, BOAZ CAME TO INSPECT THE WORK. IT WAS GOD'S PLAN THAT RUTH WAS IN THE FIELD THAT DAY.

BOAZ GREETED THE HEAD WORKER IN THE NAME OF GOD.

BOAZ SPOKE TO ALL THE WORKERS KINDLY.

197

RUTH SAW HOW GIVING AND CARING BOAZ WAS AND FELL IN LOVE WITH HIM.

Who is that girl?

That is the Moabite girl, who is the daughter-in-law of your kinsmen.

Very impressive.

BOAZ SAW RUTH WORKING HARD IN THE FIELDS.

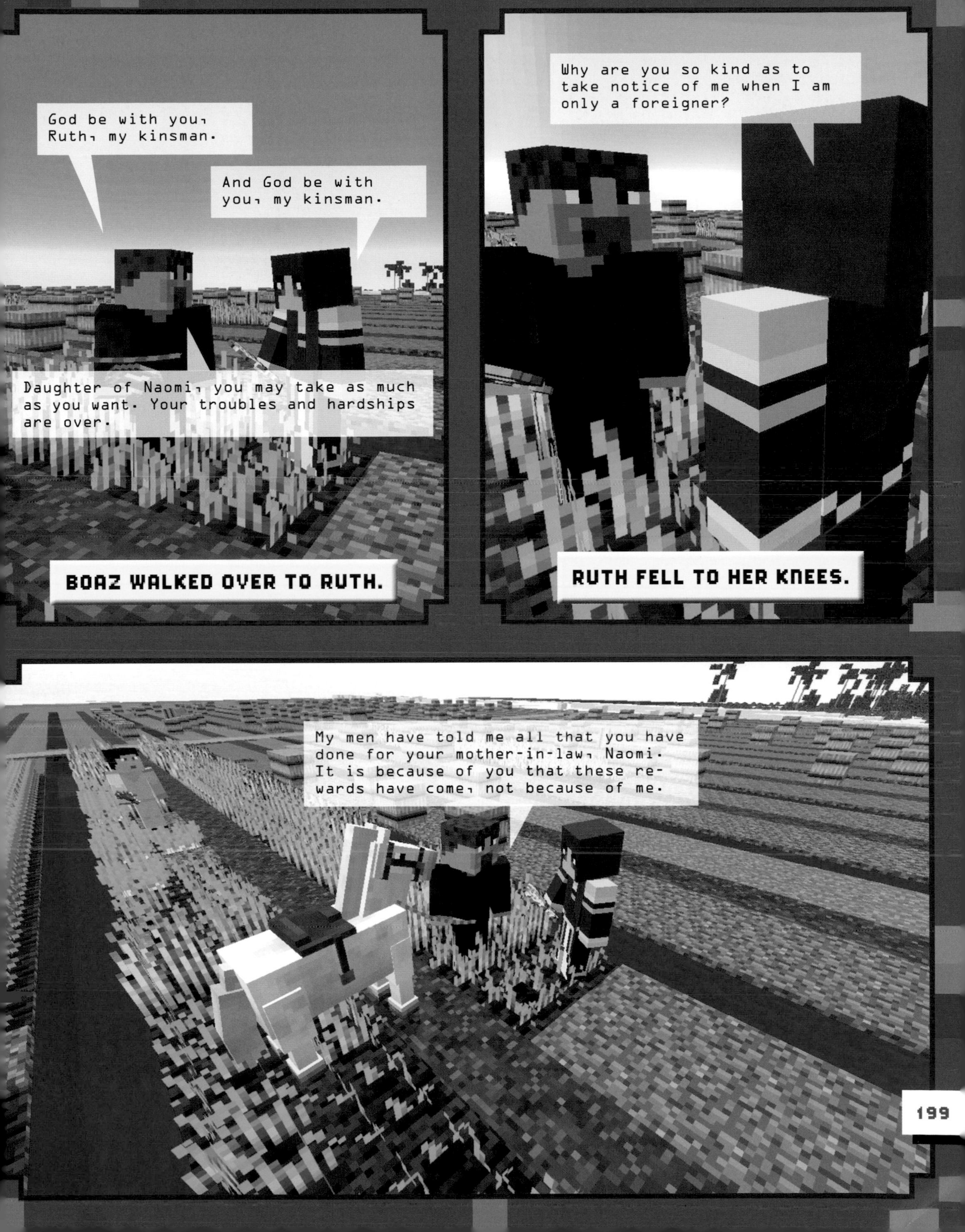
God be with you, Ruth, my kinsman.
And God be with you, my kinsman.
Daughter of Naomi, you may take as much as you want. Your troubles and hardships are over.
BOAZ WALKED OVER TO RUTH.
Why are you so kind as to take notice of me when I am only a foreigner?
RUTH FELL TO HER KNEES.
My men have told me all that you have done for your mother-in-law, Naomi. It is because of you that these rewards have come, not because of me.

BOAZ THEN TOLD HIS MEN TO PULL OUT THE BEST OF THE CROPS AND LEAVE THEM FOR RUTH.

NAOMI COULD NOT BELIEVE THE AMOUNT OF FOOD RUTH BROUGHT HOME.

Boaz instructed the workers to leave the best of his crops for me so that we may have enough food to eat. I love him!

I have prayed to the Lord to see you happy once more. Go to Boaz tonight. The Lord will guide your actions.

BOAZ WAS CELEBRATING HIS HARVEST AT A PARTY.

BOAZ AND RUTH SAW EACH OTHER AT THE SAME TIME, AND WHEN THEIR EYES MET, THEY BOTH KNEW THAT THEY LOVED ONE ANOTHER.

THAT NIGHT, BOAZ PROPOSED TO RUTH. SHORTLY AFTER, THEY WERE MARRIED.

THE LORD THEN BLESSED RUTH AND BOAZ WITH A SON. THEY NAMED HIM OBED.

OBED WAS THE FATHER
OF JESSE, AND JESSE
WAS THE FATHER OF
DAVID, THE KING OF
ISRAEL, AND ANCESTOR
OF JESUS THE CHRIST.

PHILISTINES
CAPTURE THE ARK

AS TEMPERS FLARED BETWEEN THE GROUPS, THE ISRAELITES WENT OUT TO FIGHT AGAINST THE PHILISTINES.

A FURIOUS BATTLE ENSUED, BUT THE PHILISTINES' NUMBERS WERE TOO GREAT, WHICH FORCED ISRAEL TO RETREAT.

Why has this happened?

THE MEN RETURNED TO CAMP DEFEATED, LOOKING TOWARD THEIR ELDERS FOR ANSWERS.

A GROUP OF SOLDIERS WERE COMMISSIONED TO SHILOH TO RETRIEVE THE ARK.

Take heart, my friends. we will send you to Shiloh.

THE SOLDIERS CAREFULLY MOVED THE ARK ACROSS THE LAND LEAD BY ELI'S TWO SONS.

Hooray!

Ahh!

Yay!

WHEN THE ARK CAME INTO CAMP, ALL THE ISRAELITE SOLDIERS SHOUTED SO LOUD THE GROUND SHOOK BENEATH THEIR FEET.

We are doomed.

This is bad.

We are now going to lose!

WHEN THE PHILISTINES HEARD THAT THE ARK HAD COME TO THE ISRAELITES' CAMP, THEY BECAME AFRAID.

THE PHILISTINES' GENERAL RALLIED HIS MEN.

Be strong, Philistines! Be men.

ONCE AGAIN, THE PHILISTINES MET THE ISRAELITES ON THE BATTLEFIELD. THEY CHARGED FORTH WITH GREATER CONFIDENCE KNOWING THE SACRED ARK WAS WITH THEM, BUT THAT CONFIDENCE WOULD SOON BE SHATTERED.

208

WHEN IT BEGAN TO LOOK LIKE THE ISRAELITES MIGHT LOSE, A BENJAMITE RAN FROM THE BATTLE TO REPORT NEWS TO SHILOH.

My heart fears for the Ark.

ELI WAS SITTING BY THE SIDE OF THE ROAD.

ELI STOPPED THE RUNNER ON HIS WAY TO SEE THE TOWN ELDERS.

You there, tell me the news.

Sadly, Israel was forced to flee again. I'm sorry, but your two sons have fallen in battle.

And the Ark was captured.

ON HEARING THE NEWS, ELI COLLAPSED, DEAD.

THE PHILISTINES TOOK THE ARK TO A TEMPLE IN ASHDOD.

THEY PLACED THE ARK IN THEIR TEMPLE OF DAGON IN FRONT OF THE GREAT STATUE.

WHEN THE PEOPLE AWOKE THE NEXT DAY, THEY FOUND DAGON HAD FALLEN OVER ON THE ARK.

BY NIGHTFALL, SOLDIERS HAD RETURNED DAGON BACK TO HIS UPRIGHT POSITION.

THE NEXT MORNING, SOLDIERS MARCHED TO THE TEMPLE TO INSPECT DAGON AND THE ARK.

ONCE AGAIN, THE SOLDIERS FOUND DAGON HAD FALLEN OVER, THIS TIME WITH CRACKS SO SEVERE, THEY FEARED ITS HEAD WOULD CRUMBLE IF THEY MOVED IT.

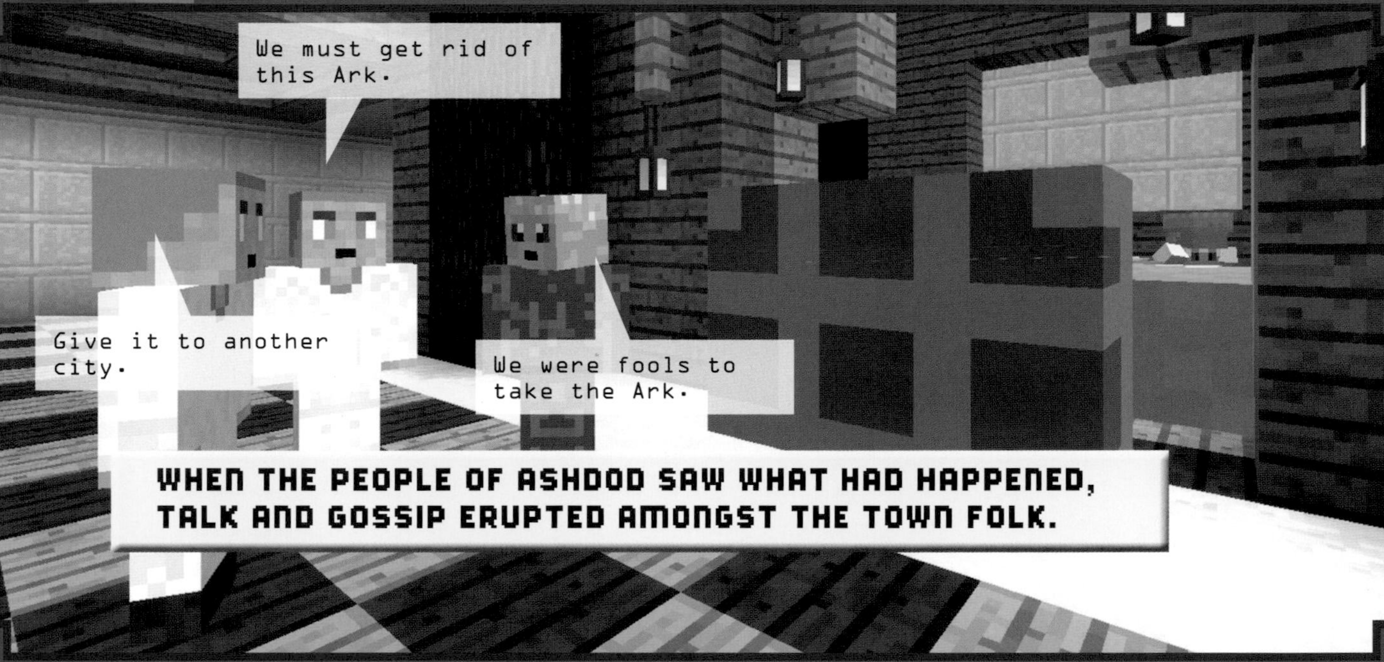
We must get rid of this Ark.
Give it to another city.
We were fools to take the Ark.
WHEN THE PEOPLE OF ASHDOD SAW WHAT HAD HAPPENED, TALK AND GOSSIP ERUPTED AMONGST THE TOWN FOLK.

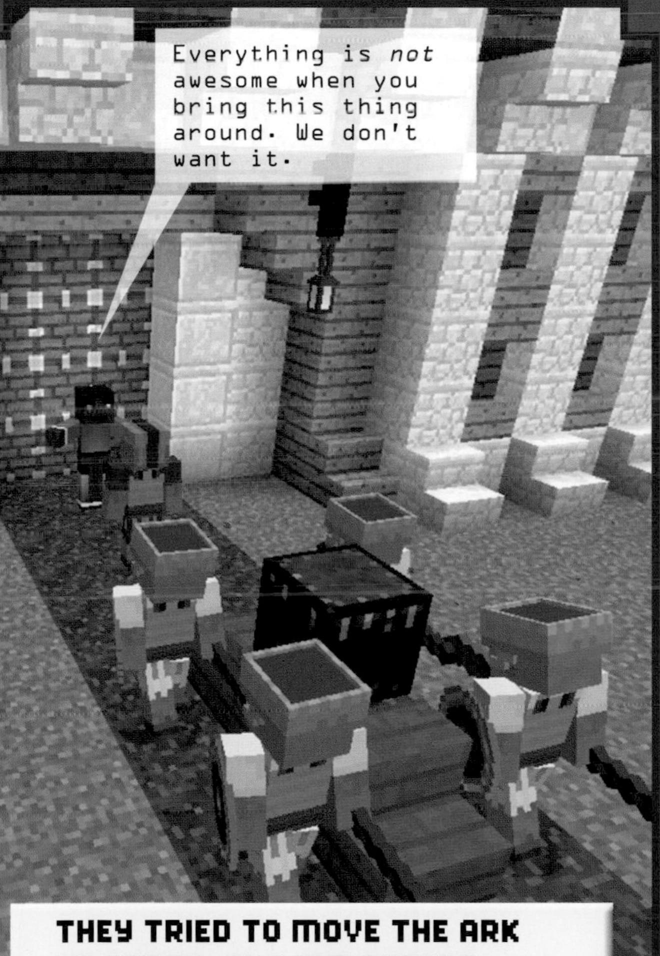
Everything is *not* awesome when you bring this thing around. We don't want it.
THEY TRIED TO MOVE THE ARK TO ETRON, BUT THE PEOPLE THERE DID NOT WANT IT, EITHER.

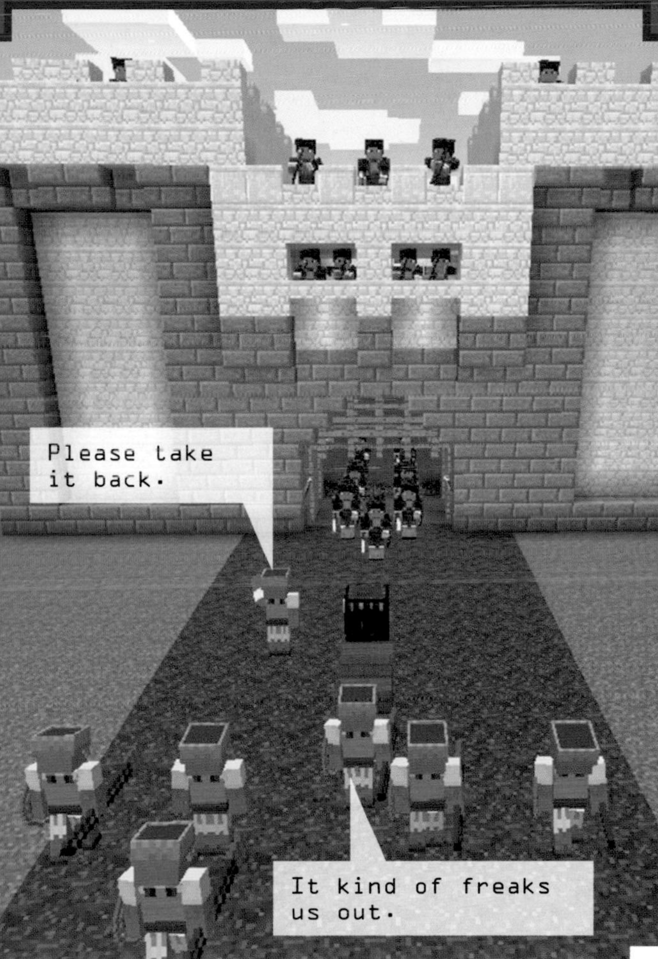
Please take it back.
It kind of freaks us out.
SO THE PHILISTINES RETURNED THE ARK TO THE ISRAELITES.

A KING FOR ISRAEL

You, my sons, shall now rule over Israel and follow in my path.

WHEN SAMUEL GREW OLD, HE APPOINTED HIS SONS AS LEADERS OF ISRAEL.

BUT HIS SONS DID NOT FOLLOW GOD'S PATH IN THEIR RULINGS.

Samuel's sons are the most dishonest men in Israel.

I hope we get the judgment we want.

Don't worry. They take bribes.

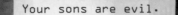

Your sons are evil.

They do not follow God.

SOON, THE TOWN LEADERS CAME TO SAMUEL.

We need a proper king.

Yes, like all the other nations around us.

THAT EVENING, SAMUEL PRAYED TO GOD, AND THE LORD INSTRUCTED HIM HOW TO PROCEED.

Lord, the people ask for a king.

They have rejected Me as their King. They have forsaken Me and served other gods. Listen to them, but warn them of what a king is like, and how they will suffer.

You do not know what you are asking for.

Just do it!

SAMUEL TRIED TO WARN THE PEOPLE, BUT THEY WOULD NOT LISTEN.

Give us a king.

We want a king.

A king will take all you have!

WHEN SAMUEL HEARD ALL THE DETERMINATION OF THE PEOPLE, HE WENT TO THE HOLY OF HOLIES AND SPOKE BEFORE GOD.

I am at a loss. The people still ask for a king even after the warning.

Listen to them and give them a king!

THERE WAS A BENJAMITE, SAUL, WHO WAS VERY HANDSOME. HE WAS TALL AND STRONG, TOO.

Now listen to me. Go out into the wild and find the donkey.

I will, father.

ONE DAY, A DONKEY BELONGING TO SAUL'S FATHER, KISH, WENT MISSING.

SO SAUL AND HIS SERVANT JOURNEYED ACROSS THE LANDS AND PASSED THROUGH THE HILL COUNTRY, INTO BENJAMIN TERRITORY.

Have courage, my good man.

Master, we are journeying into lands we do not know.

There is a man of God in that town who can tell us where the donkey is.

Let's head back. We are so far from home. We will never find that donkey.

WHILE SAMUEL WAS SITTING OUTSIDE HIS HOUSE, GOD SPOKE TO HIM.

A man will come to you and ask for a donkey he lost. Anoint him ruler over Israel.

217

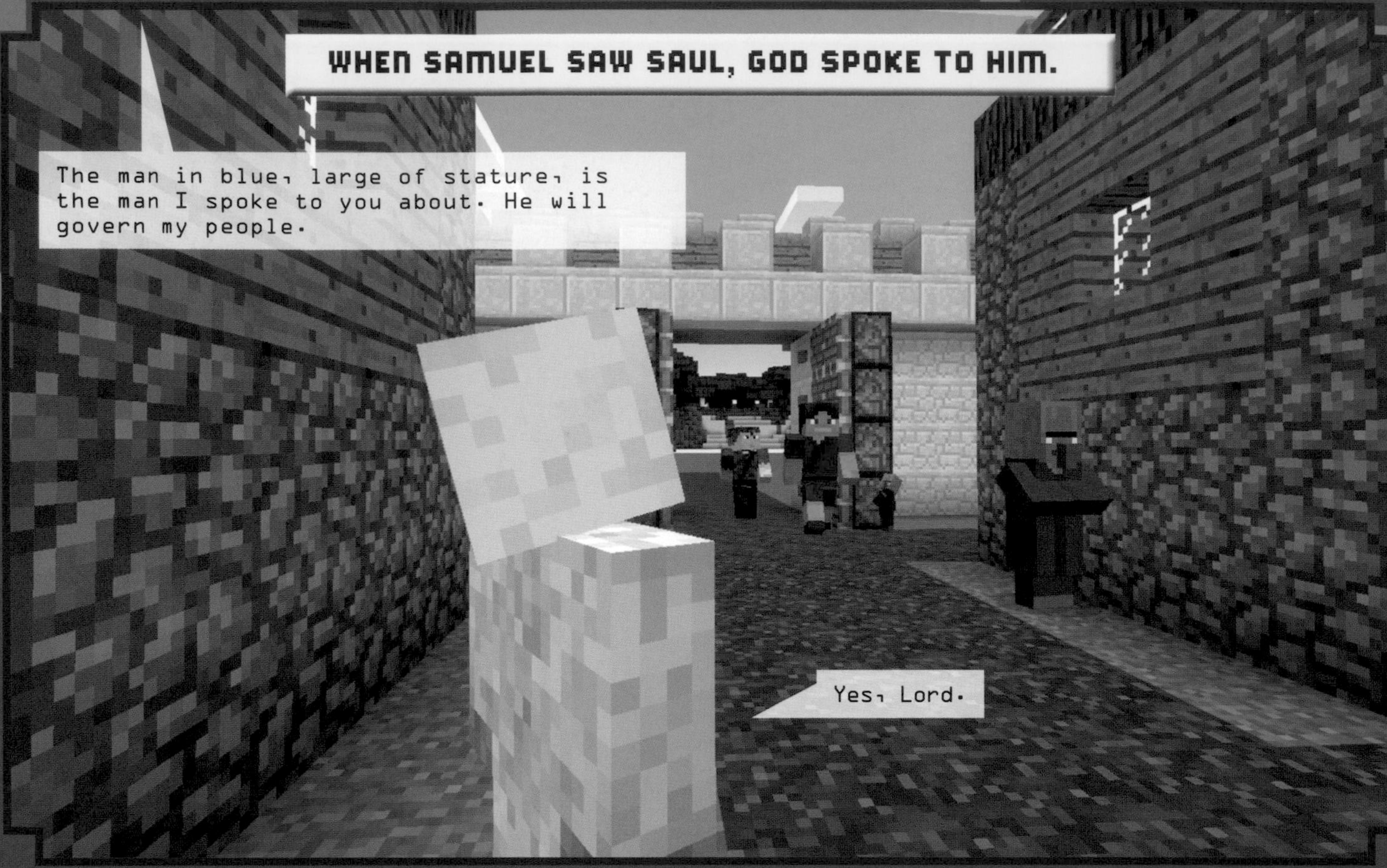
WHEN SAMUEL SAW SAUL, GOD SPOKE TO HIM.
The man in blue, large of stature, is the man I spoke to you about. He will govern my people.
Yes, Lord.

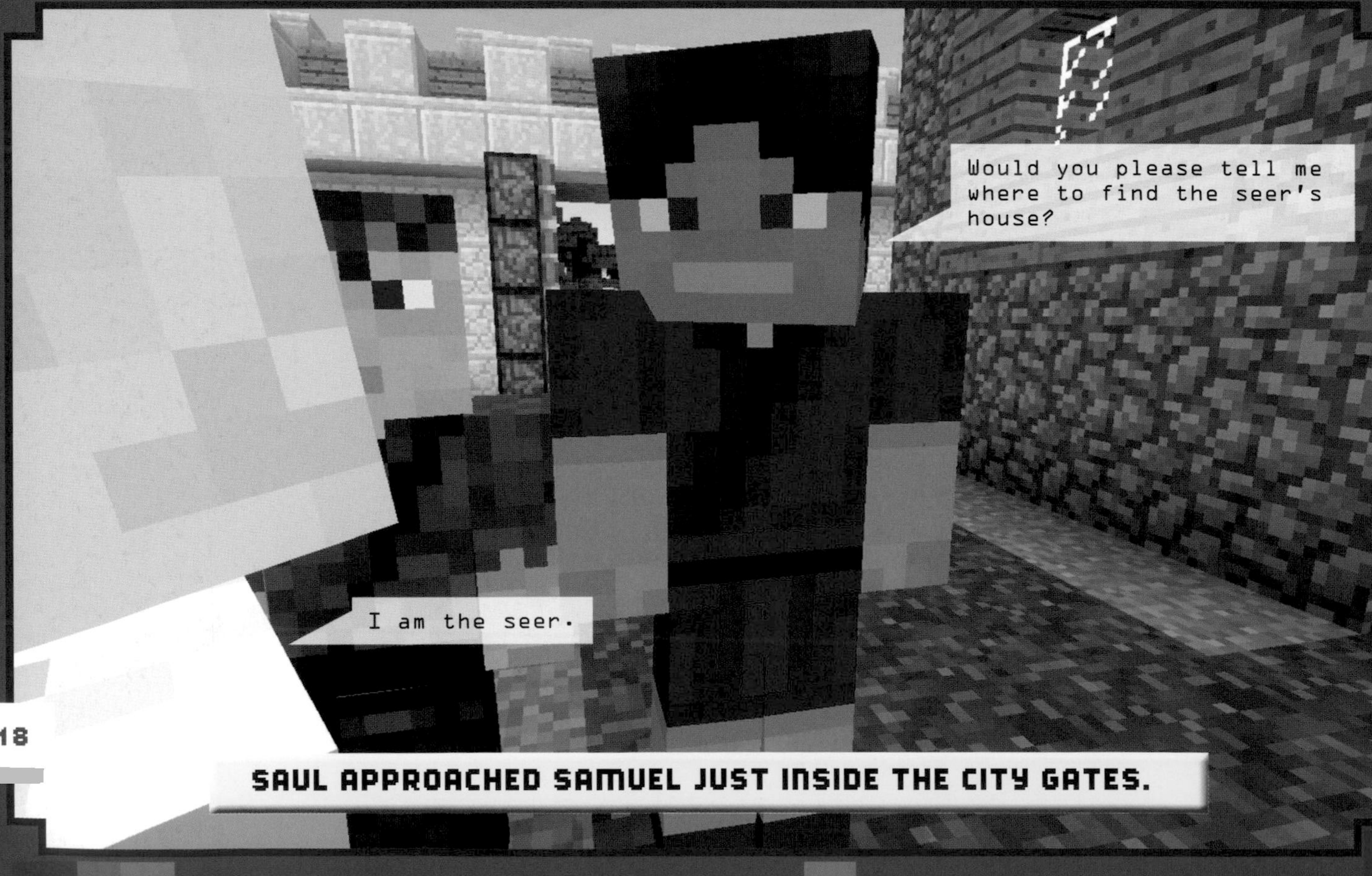
Would you please tell me where to find the seer's house?
I am the seer.
SAUL APPROACHED SAMUEL JUST INSIDE THE CITY GATES.

Head to my quarters up
the hill. Today you will
eat with me.

Thank you. That is
very kind of you.

As for the donkey,
it has been found.

Whoa! You really are a seer.

Let us be served,
but first, we must
give thanks.

219

SAMUEL BROUGHT SAUL TO HIS HOUSE AND
SEATED HIM AT THE HEAD OF THE TABLE.

God delivered you to me. He has big plans for you.

AFTER DINNER, SAMUEL TALKED WITH SAUL ON THE ROOF OF HIS HOUSE.

The Lord has anointed you ruler over His inheritance, as I anoint you now with this oil.

SAMUEL TOOK A FLASK OF OLIVE OIL AND POURED IT ON SAUL'S HEAD.

When you leave me, you will be given these signs as proof that God has anointed you king of all of Israel: First, you will meet two men near Rachel's tomb, and they will tell you the donkey is found. Then, at the great tree of Tabor, men will break bread with you, and finally, at Gibeath, you will meet prophets, a sign that the spirit of the Lord is with you.

"YOU WILL MEET TWO MEN NEAR THE TOMB OF RACHEL. THEY WILL TELL YOU ABOUT THE DONKEY."

Aren't you Saul? Your father's donkey has been found.

"NEXT, YOU WILL MEET THREE MEN AT THE TREE OF TABOR AND EAT WITH THEM."

Welcome, friend. Will you join us for breakfast?

"AFTER THAT, YOU WILL GO TO GIBEATH AND MEET PROPHETS.

We've been expecting you. The Lord told us you would be coming.

"THE SPIRIT OF THE LORD WILL COME POWERFULLY UPON YOU, AND YOU WILL BE A DIFFERENT MAN."

The Lord blesses this man.

SAUL MADE KING

Take these letters to the leaders of all the tribes of Israel. I have urgent news.

SAMUEL SUMMONED THE PEOPLE OF ISRAEL TO PRESENT THEMSELVES TO THE LORD.

THE TRIBES SOON GATHERED, AND SAMUEL SPOKE TO THE PEOPLE.

I will find you a king. Gather in your tribes, and present yourselves before the Lord so He can pick one of you.

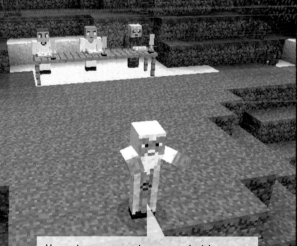

You have spoken and the Lord has answered....

According to the lot, the king will come from the tribe of the Benjamites.

SAMUEL HAD ALL OF THE BENJAMITES COME FORWARD.

THEN HE PULLED A BENJAMITE FROM THE CROWD.

You there, come forward. God has spoken, and your offspring will be the chosen one to lead Israel.

KISH WAS BROUGHT FORWARD.

Saul, son of Kish, has been chosen by God to be the king of Israel.

THE PEOPLE CALLED OUT FOR THEIR NEW KING.

Where is he?

Bring us our king.

THE LORD ANSWERED

He is hidden among the supplies.

Go get him.

THEY FOUND SAUL AMONG THE SUPPLIES.

225

WHEN SAUL FINALLY STEPPED
OUT OF HIDING, HE WAS A FOOT
TALLER THAN ALL THE OTHER
ISRAELITES.

Do you see the man that the
Lord has chosen? There is no
one like him in all of Israel.
He shall be the answer to
your pleas.

Long live the king!

SAMUEL HAD THE SCRIBES WRITE
DOWN THE DUTIES OF THE KING
AND HANDED THEM TO SAUL.

NOT SOON AFTER, NAHASH, THE RULER OF THE AMMONITES, BESIEGED THE CITY OF JABESH GILEAD.

THE ELDERS OF JABESH ASKED NAHASH TO GIVE THEM MORE TIME. IN THAT TIME, THEY HOPED TO GET HELP.

If you give us seven days and no one comes to our aid, we will become your servants.

No one will come.

Oh, no!

What is going on?

Send a message to all of Israel that Saul commands them to follow him into battle against Nahash and the Ammonites.

THEY TOLD SAUL WHAT HAPPENED TO THE CITY OF JABESH.

So this is why everyone is weeping.

THEN, THE SPIRIT OF THE LORD FELL ONTO THE PEOPLE AND THEY CAME TOGETHER AS ONE UNDER SAUL.

THE NEXT DAY, THE ISRAELITES ATTACKED THE AMMONITES AND WON A GREAT BATTLE.

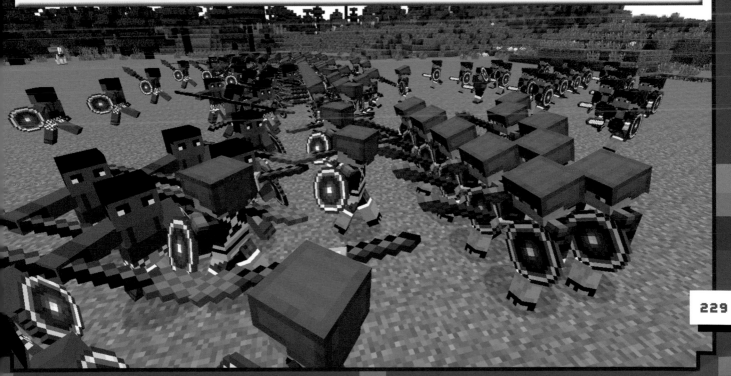

Take a group of our finest soldiers and attack Gebe.

As you command, father.

YEARS AFTER HIS GREAT VICTORY, SAUL SENT HIS SON, JONATHAN, TO ATTACK THE PHILISTINES AND RUN THEM OUT OF THE LAND OF ISRAEL.

UNDER THE COVER OF NIGHT, JONATHAN AND HIS MEN CAME UPON THE PHILISTINES.

Climb quickly!

ONCE INSIDE, THEY FOUGHT THEIR WAY ACROSS THE WALL.

To the gate.

AFTER SWIFTLY RELEASING THE GATE, THE ISRAELITES RUSHED IN AND TOOK THE OUTPOST.

War! War! War!

IN RETALIATION, THE PHILISTINES ASSEMBLED THEIR ARMY.

WHEN THE ISRAELITES SAW HOW STRONG THE PHILISTINES WERE, THEY RAN AND HID IN CAVES AND THICKETS.

SAMUEL GAVE COUNCIL TO SAUL.

Call the men back, and in seven days, I will come and give sacrifice.

SAUL ORDERED ALL THE SOLDIERS BACK TO CAMP.

What am I going to do? The men are getting scared again.

BUT SEVEN DAYS PASSED AND SAMUEL DID NOT COME.

SAUL DECIDED, AS KING, TO ACT IN SAMUEL'S STEAD.

You're late.

A prophet is never late, nor is he early. He arrives precisely when he means to. What have you done?

JUST THEN, SAMUEL ARRIVED.

The men were scared and you didn't come so I gave the burnt offering.

You foolish man! Once again, you are not keeping to the Lord's commands.

If you will not follow the Lord, your kingship over Israel will end.

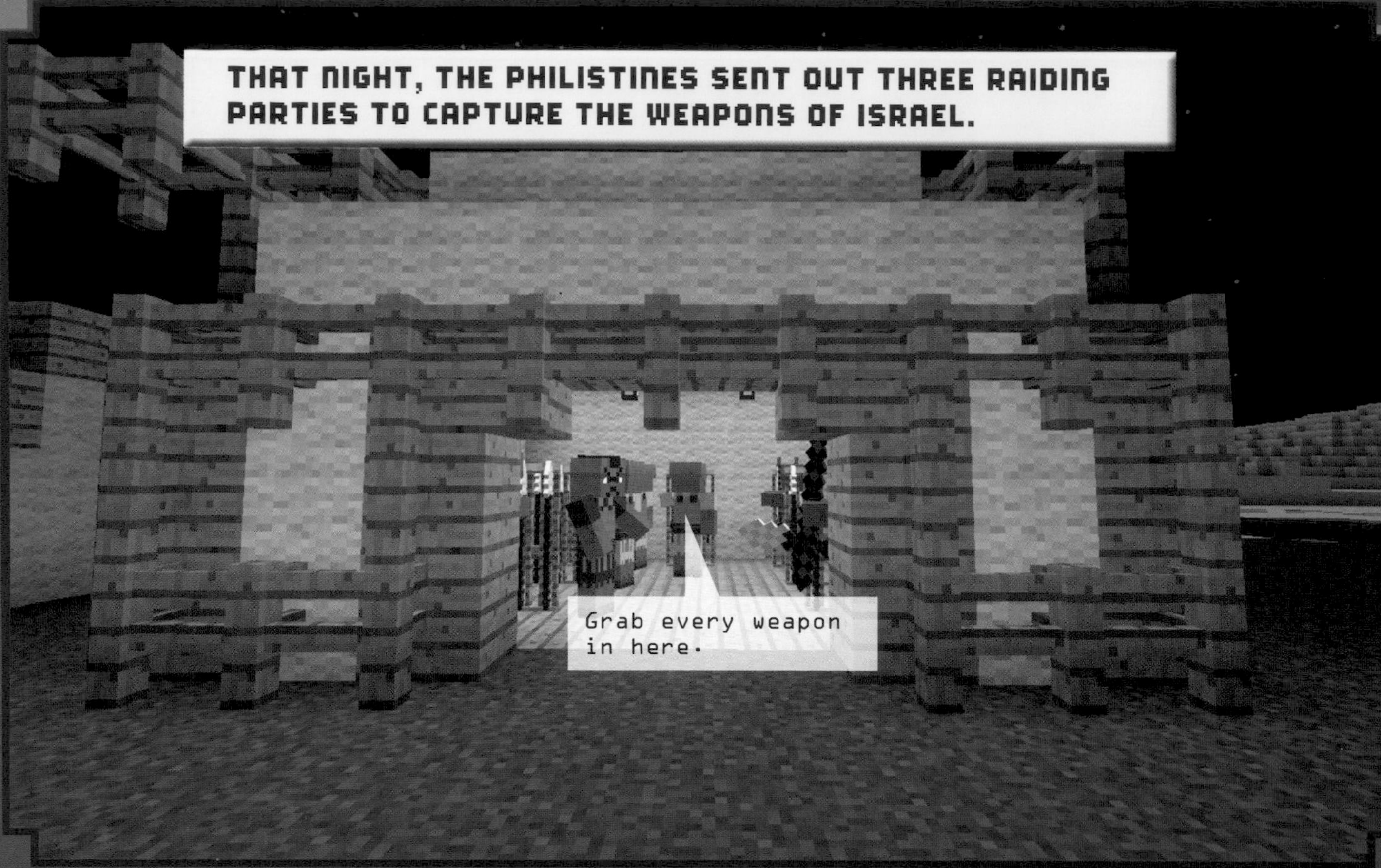
THAT NIGHT, THE PHILISTINES SENT OUT THREE RAIDING PARTIES TO CAPTURE THE WEAPONS OF ISRAEL.
Grab every weapon in here.

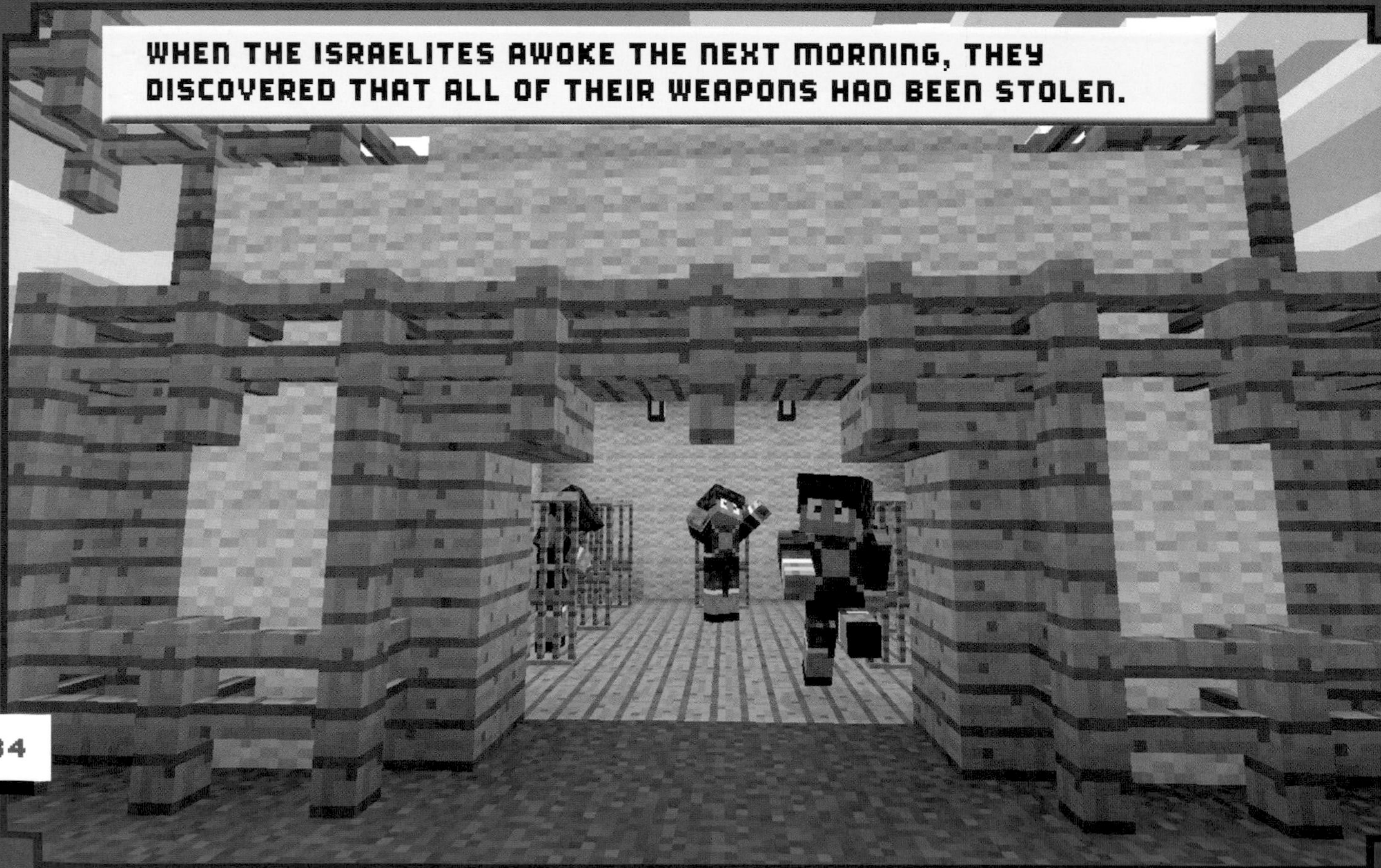
WHEN THE ISRAELITES AWOKE THE NEXT MORNING, THEY DISCOVERED THAT ALL OF THEIR WEAPONS HAD BEEN STOLEN.

JONATHAN CALLED HIS TOP SWORDSMAN TO JOIN HIM.

THEY CREPT OUT OF CAMP.

THEY CLIMBED VERY HIGH.

THEY CLIMBED A CLIFF TO GET TO THE PHILISTINE OUTPOST.

UPON REACHING THE PLATEAU, THE PHILISTINES SAW JONATHAN AND RUSHED OUT TO ATTACK HIM.

AS BEFORE, THE PHILISTINES FELL TO JONATHAN'S BLADE.

235

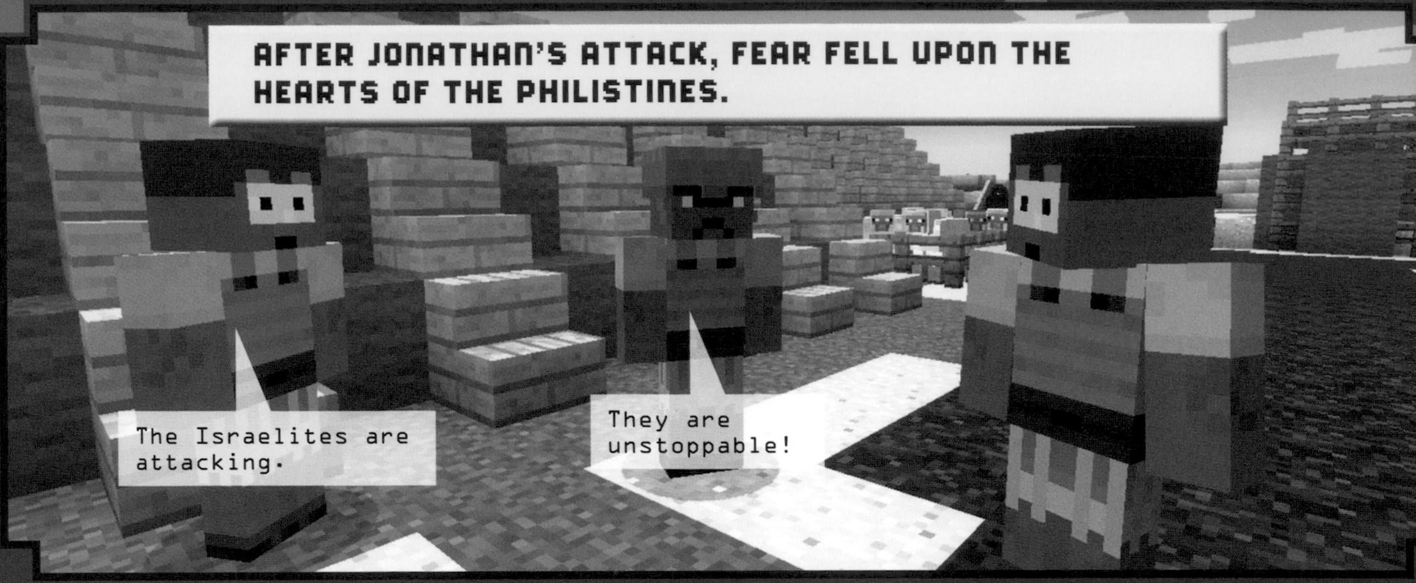
AFTER JONATHAN'S ATTACK, FEAR FELL UPON THE HEARTS OF THE PHILISTINES.
The Israelites are attacking.
They are unstoppable!

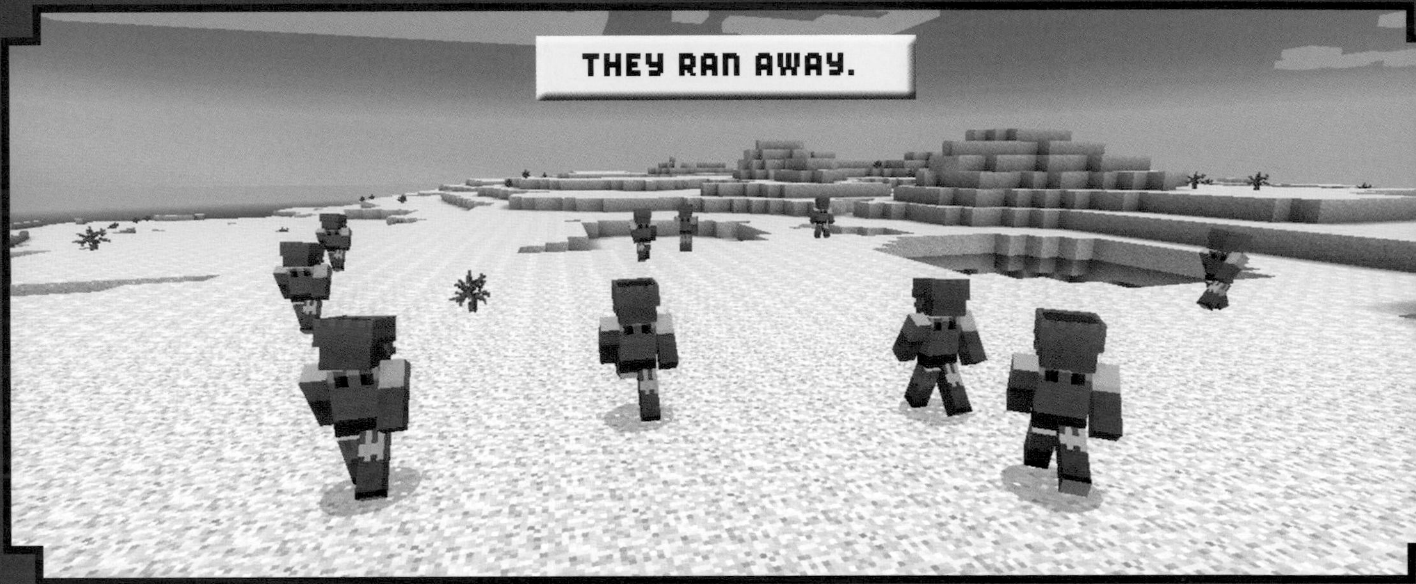
THEY RAN AWAY.

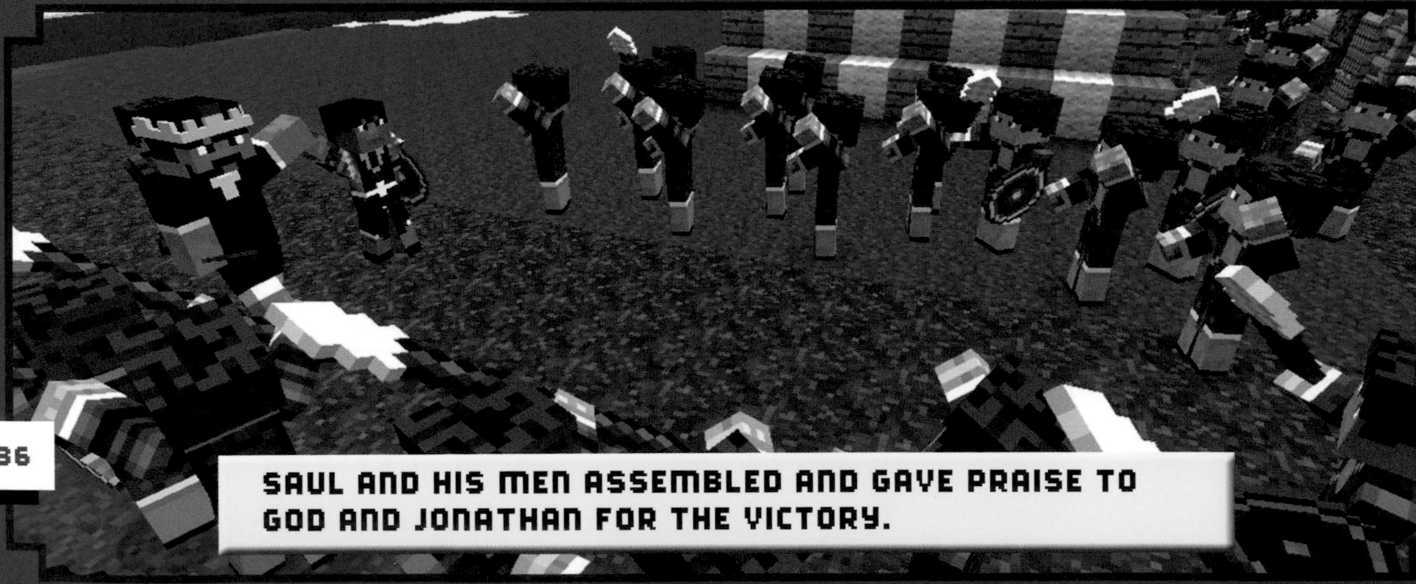
SAUL AND HIS MEN ASSEMBLED AND GAVE PRAISE TO GOD AND JONATHAN FOR THE VICTORY.

EVEN AFTER ALL OF SAUL'S VICTORIES, ENEMIES CONTINUED TO COME FORWARD AGAINST ISRAEL. SOON, IT WAS THE AMALEKITES WHO CAME TO ATTACK.

SAMUEL APPROACHED SAUL WITH THE WORD OF GOD.

I must attack the Amalekites to save God's people.

I am the one who anointed you king. You ignore my commandments, yet I forgive you. You must heed my word this time.

God commands that you cannot take anything from the Amalekites. Obey God or suffer His wrath.

I order the people to war. We must protect ourselves.

SAUL ASSEMBLED AN ARMY AND ATTACKED THE AMALEKITES.

TAKING INVENTORY OF THE SPOILS OF HIS VICTORY, SAUL WALKED TO THE CITY, LUSTING IN HIS HEART FOR THE WEALTH THAT LAY AROUND HIM.

Bring me all the best cattle and sheep. Also, bring any other riches.

But, God said we are not to. This is a great sin to go against God.

I don't care. Do as I say.

Saul has disobeyed me for the last time. I regret making him king. I shall raise another up as king.

Saul.

I have done what the Lord ordered.

What is this I hear of you taking sheep and cattle?

Well, yes, but I took them because they are worth so much. I didn't think god would mind if I used them for Godly purposes.

Enough. The Lord sent you on a mission to destroy all of the Amalekites. You did not destroy everything. Why do you not obey God?

I wanted to please my men—but I was going to sacrifice the animals.

You are a fool. The Lord delights much more in us obeying His commandments than in burnt offering.

A humble heart that obeys the Lord is what God loves. The Lord has torn Israel from you today.

SAMUEL TURNED TO LEAVE, AND AS SAUL REACHED OUT TO STOP HIM, HE TORE A PIECE OF SAMUEL'S ROBE. THAT SMALL FABRIC IS ALL THAT REMAINED OF SAUL'S POSESSIONS.

DAVID AND GOLIATH

It's time the Hebrews had
a formal leader.

THE STORY OF KING DAVID BEGINS WHEN HE WAS A YOUNG MAN. DAVID WAS THE YOUNGEST OF EIGHT BROTHERS, AND HIS JOB WAS TO LOOK AFTER HIS FATHER'S FLOCK.

A STORY IS TOLD OF HOW A LION ONCE ATTACKED THE FLOCK DAVID WAS WATCHING. THE LION GRABBED A LAMB AND TRIED TO MAKE OFF WITH IT. DAVID SHOWED NO FEAR AND ATTACKED THE LION WITH A SLING AND STONE.

Take that, you wild beast! I will not let you hurt any of my sheep.

THE PEOPLE OF ISRAEL ASKED GOD TO GIVE THEM A KING SO THAT THEY COULD BE LIKE THE OTHER PEOPLES OF THE WORLD. GOD APPOINTED THE PROPHET SAMUEL TO ANOINT SAUL AS THE FIRST KING OF ISRAEL. SAUL RULED WITH INJUSTICE, SO GOD TOLD THE PROPHET SAMUEL THAT DAVID WOULD BE THE NEW KING.

WHEN SAMUEL ARRIVED IN BETHLEHEM, HE WENT TO DAVID'S FATHER, JESSE. JESSE SHOWED SAMUEL HIS TWO ELDEST SONS.

Please bring David to me.

He is my youngest. How could the Lord choose him as king?

SAMUEL ANOINTED DAVID IN THE NAME OF THE LORD, KING OF ALL ISRAEL.

Guard, go and find me a minstrel who can play sweet music. I need it to soothe my soul.

THE LORD REMOVED HIS BLESSINGS FROM SAUL BECAUSE OF ALL THE WICKED THINGS HE DID WHILE KING. THIS CAUSED SAUL TO FEEL BAD.

Hang in there, my King— things will get better.

ONE OF THE ADVISORS KNEW OF A YOUNG MAN WHO COULD PLAY THE HARP MORE BEAUTIFULLY THAN ANY OTHER PERSON. HE SAID THAT THE LORD HAD BLESSED HIM WITH A GIFT OF DIVINE MUSIC. SAUL CALLED FOR THAT BOY.

Greetings, my King. Would you like me to begin?

SAUL WAS ON HIS THRONE WHEN THE BOY ARRIVED WITH HIS HARP.

DAVID'S MUSIC WAS SO SOOTHING THAT IT HELPED SAUL FORGET ABOUT HIS TROUBLES. SAUL PRAISED DAVID AND MADE HIM A KING'S HELPER.

247

DURING DAVID'S TIME, THE NEIGHBORS OF ISRAEL WERE THE PHILISTINES. ISRAEL AND THE PHILISTINES ALWAYS FOUGHT. TROUBLE ONCE AGAIN CAME TO ISRAEL AND THE PHILISTINES ATTACKED. ALL THE SONS OF ISRAEL WERE CALLED OUT TO MILITARY SERVICE.

EACH ARMY HELD THEIR GROUND ON OPPOSITE SIDES OF A DRIED RIVERBED.

IN THE ANCIENT TRADITION, THE ISRAELITES COULD SEND OUT A CHAMPION TO COMBAT AGAINST THE PHILISTINE CHAMPION. IF THE CHAMPION WON, THE DEFEATED ARMY WOULD SURRENDER TO THE ISRAELITES, AND VICE VERSA.

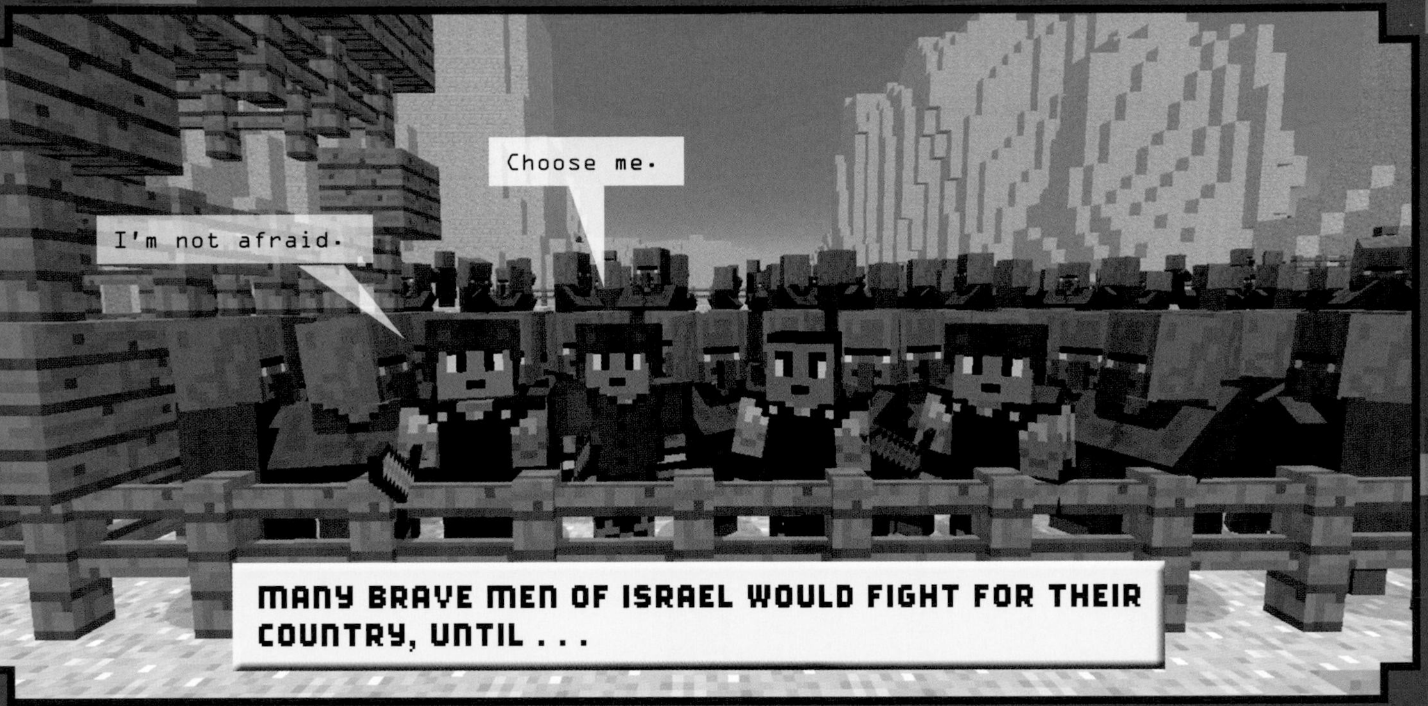
I'm not afraid.
Choose me.
MANY BRAVE MEN OF ISRAEL WOULD FIGHT FOR THEIR COUNTRY, UNTIL . . .

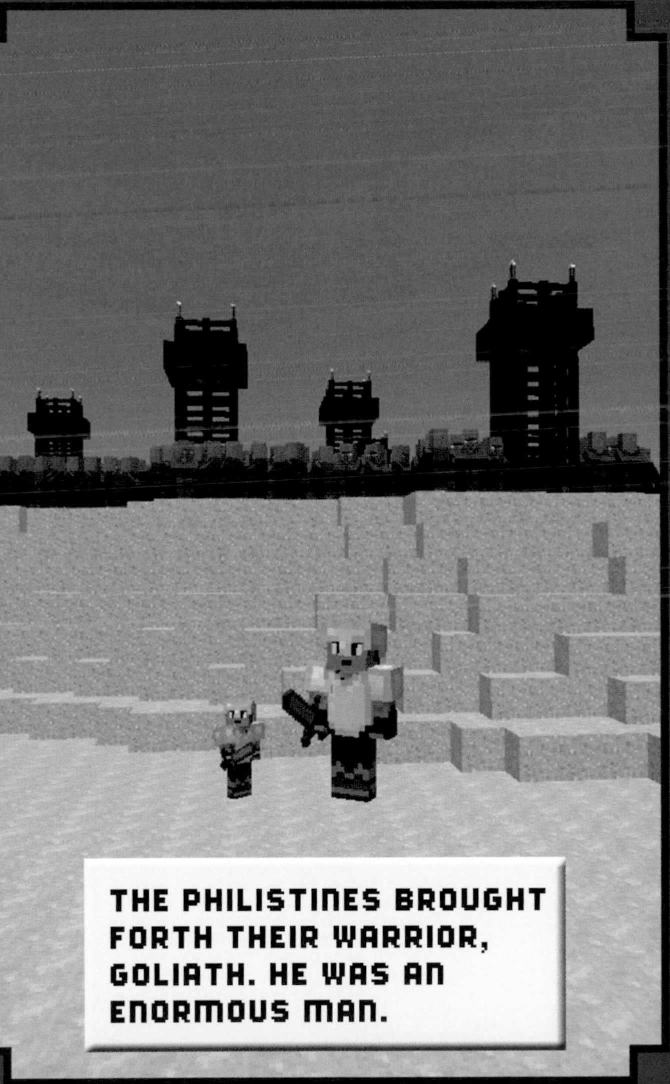
THE PHILISTINES BROUGHT FORTH THEIR WARRIOR, GOLIATH. HE WAS AN ENORMOUS MAN.

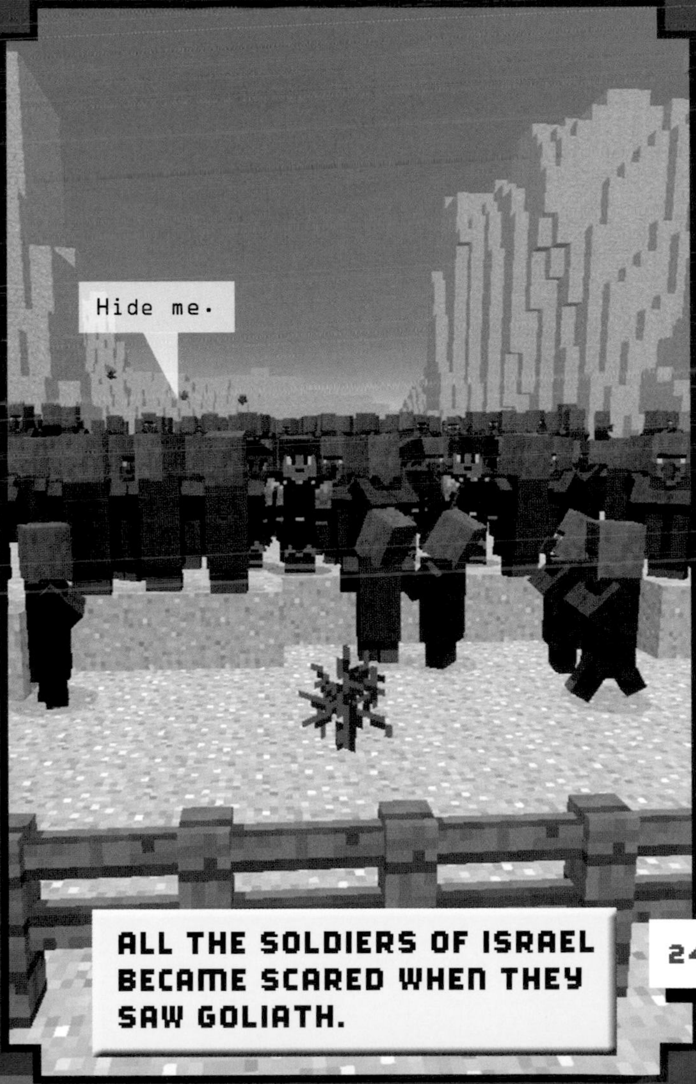
Hide me.
ALL THE SOLDIERS OF ISRAEL BECAME SCARED WHEN THEY SAW GOLIATH.

FOR FORTY DAYS, NO ONE WOULD STEP FORWARD FOR THE ISRAELITES, UNTIL ONE DAY, LITTLE DAVID WENT TO THE FRONT LINES.

You are only a boy, and Goliath has been a fighting man all his life.

I am a shepherd and have killed lions and bears with only a sling. I will win this battle.

SAUL THEN SENT FOR DAVID.

HE TOOK HIS SLING TO BATTLE.

251

DAVID WAS NOT AFRAID.

GOLIATH MOVED TOWARD DAVID.

DAVID FLUNG THE STONE THROUGH THE AIR WITH ALL OF GOD'S MIGHT, AND STRUCK GOLIATH IN THE HEAD.

THE GIANT FELL TO THE GROUND, DEAD.

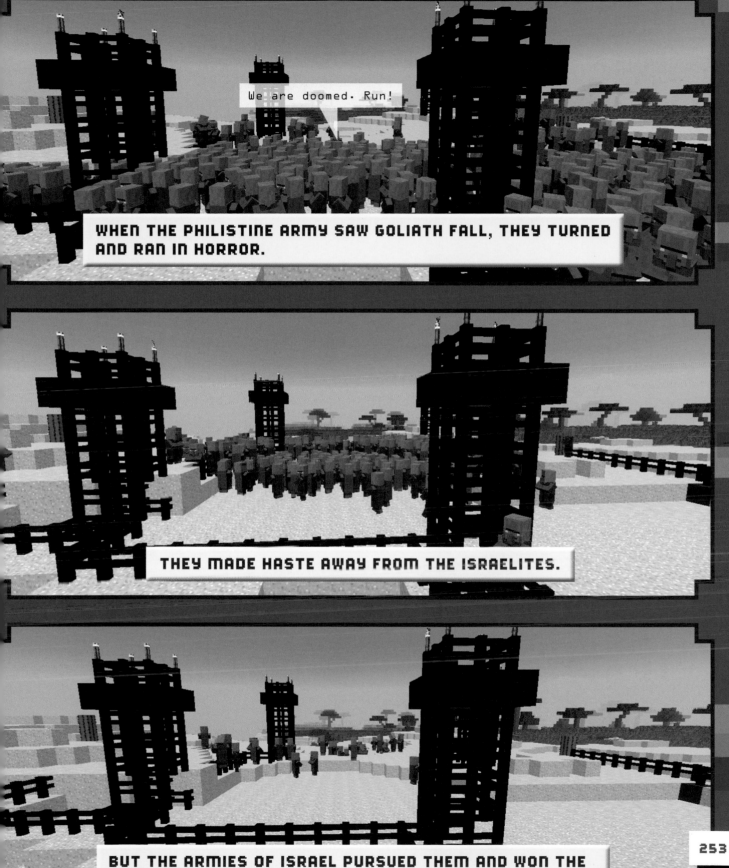

We are doomed. Run!

WHEN THE PHILISTINE ARMY SAW GOLIATH FALL, THEY TURNED AND RAN IN HORROR.

THEY MADE HASTE AWAY FROM THE ISRAELITES.

253

BUT THE ARMIES OF ISRAEL PURSUED THEM AND WON THE WAR THAT VERY DAY.

DAVID BECOMES KING

That was an epic takedown for someone so small!

You are plotting against me! I am the King of these lands and no one else will be until the day I die.

IN TIME, DAVID WON MANY BATTLES. KING SAUL BECAME ANGRY AT DAVID FOR HIS SUCCESS. ONE DAY, AS DAVID PLAYED THE HARP FOR SAUL, HE ATTACKED DAVID.

DAVID NARROWLY ESCAPED THE ATTACK. THAT NIGHT HE LEFT JERU-SALEM TO SEEK REFUGE FROM SAUL'S WRATH.

255

What have I done to make Saul so angry at me?

Saul has fallen out of favor with the Lord. Saul will do everything in his might to keep you from becoming king.

DAVID WENT TO THE PROPHET. DAVID DIDN'T UNDERSTAND WHY THESE THINGS WERE HAPPENING TO HIM.

To King David!

DAVID WENT TO THE CAVE OF ADULLAM. MEN OF ALL KINDS HEARD THAT DAVID WAS TAKING REFUGE IN THESE CAVES. THEY CAME TO HIM AND PLEDGED THEIR ALLEGIANCE. DAVID QUICKLY AMASSED A FOLLOWING STRONG ENOUGH TO OPPOSE SAUL.

That imposter must be brought down!

SAUL ORDERED HIS CAPTAIN TO CALL FORTH THE ISRAELITE ARMY AND HUNT DAVID DOWN.

I can't believe how foolish Saul is.

Stay here. I have a plan.

FOR MONTHS, SAUL HUNTED DAVID, BUT HE COULD NEVER FIND HIM. ONE DAY, SAUL WENT INTO THE CAVE WHERE DAVID AND HIS MEN HAD THEIR HIDEOUT. SAUL DECIDED TO REST IN THE CAVE.

Saul, you will see what a true servant of the Lord will do when his enemy is delivered into his hands.

DAVID SNUCK UP ON SAUL AND DREW HIS SWORD.

Let this be a lesson to him and all my followers.

DAVID SLASHED SAUL, BUT INSTEAD OF HURTING HIM, HE ONLY TOOK A PIECE OF SAUL'S ROBE.

WHEN SAUL LEFT THE CAVE, DAVID CAME OUT AND HELD THE PIECE OF CLOTH UP FOR ALL TO SEE. SAUL LEFT THAT DAY, KNOWING THAT HE HAD BEEN SPARED BY DAVID.

Ah, my trusty stone and sling, I call on you again.

SAUL STILL COULD NOT BE TRUSTED. DAVID'S CAPTAIN SNUCK INTO THE CAMP TO SHOW SAUL, ONCE AGAIN, THAT DAVID WAS THE ANOINTED KING OF ISRAEL.

Quiet, we will enter here.

I'm right behind you.

259

SAUL'S MEN WERE SO TIRED AFTER THEIR MARCH, THEY FELL ASLEEP. DAVID QUIETLY MADE HIS WAY INTO THE CAMP.

THEY ENTERED THE COURTYARD OF THE CAMP. THERE, IN THE MIDDLE, STOOD FOUR TOWERS WITH GUARDS, AND, BETWEEN THEM, SAUL'S MASSIVE TENT. THEY EASED ALONG THE WALL INTO SAUL'S TENT.

SAUL WAS ASLEEP. TOGETHER, DAVID AND HIS CAPTAIN TIP-TOED OVER TO SAUL'S BED. THE CAPTAIN ASKED DAVID IF HE COULD STRIKE SAUL DOWN, BUT DAVID REFUSED.

Take this, David. A man without his sword is no man.

Great idea. Let us leave quietly, so as not to be discovered. Just imagine what his face is going to look like tomorrow when I show everyone the sword.

DAVID NOTICED A CHEST.

The Lord has delivered you into my hands and yet I have spared you once again. Make peace with me, Saul.

262

IN THE MORNING, DAVID CALLED OUT TO SAUL, SHOWING ALL THAT HE HAD SAUL'S WEAPON.

SAUL WAS AT HIS WITS' END, HAVING GROWN FRUSTRATED WITH HIS ELUSIVE FOE, SO HE TURNED TO MAGIC AND SORCERY TO SOLVE HIS PROBLEMS. SAUL WENT TO A WOMAN WHO COULD CONJURE SPIRITS FROM THE DEAD, AND ASKED HER TO BRING BACK THE SPIRIT OF SAMUEL.

Saul, the Lord has departed from you and become your enemy. Your kingdom has been taken from you and given to David. The Philistines have come once more and you and all your descendants will be delivered to them. You will be no more!

263

SAUL GOT A MESSAGE, BUT IT WAS NOT WHAT HE WAS HOPING FOR. GOD WAS ANGRY.

Ahhhhh!

WHEN SAUL HEARD THIS, HE RAN AWAY IN FEAR.

SOON, SAUL AND ALL HIS SONS DIED IN A BATTLE AGAINST THE PHILISTINES.

NEWS OF THE BATTLE CAME TO DAVID. WHEN DAVID HEARD ABOUT SAUL, HE WEPT AND FASTED.

EVEN THOUGH SAUL TRIED TO KILL DAVID, HE HONORED SAUL AS THE LORD'S ANOINTED KING UNTIL THE END.

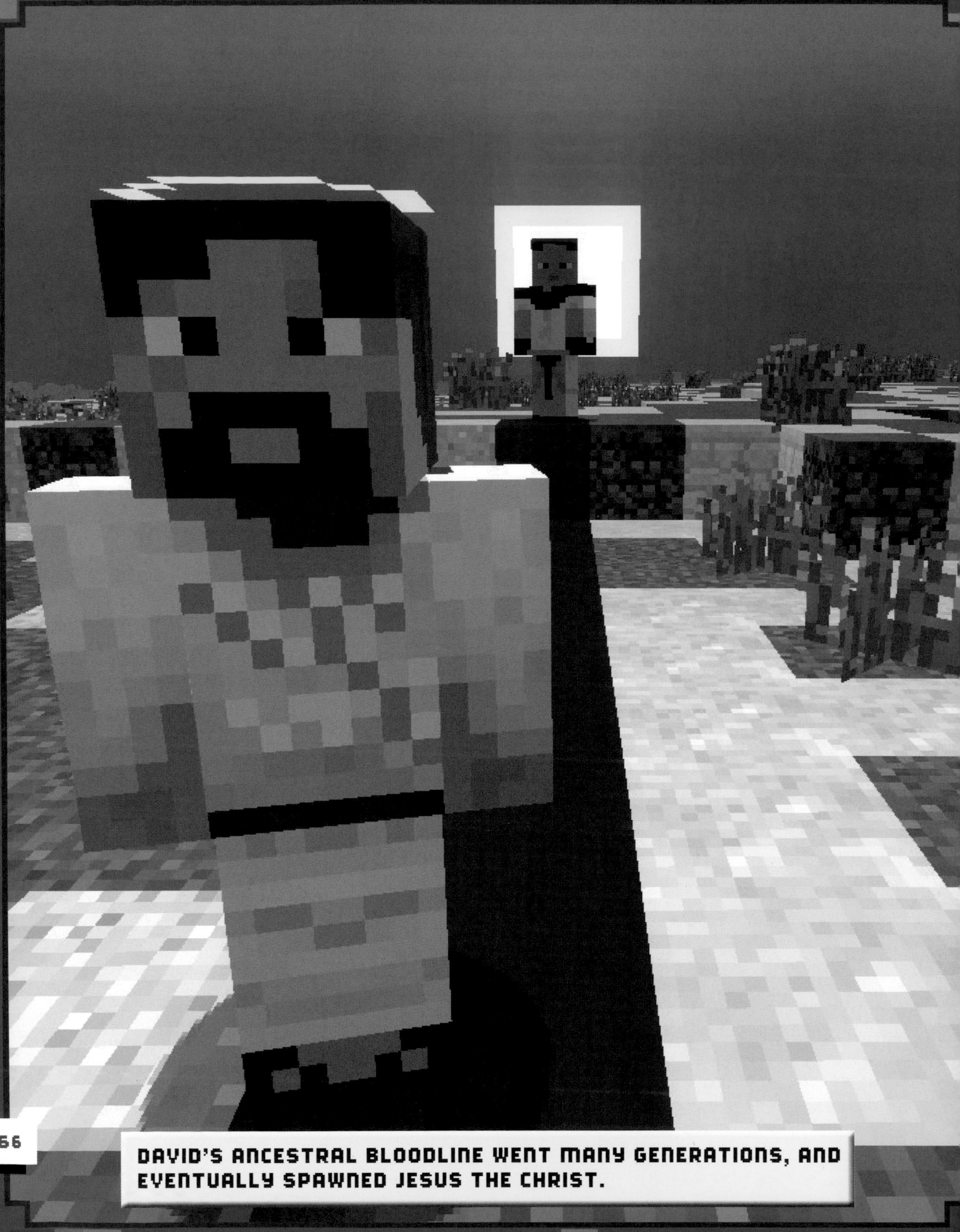

DAVID'S ANCESTRAL BLOODLINE WENT MANY GENERATIONS, AND EVENTUALLY SPAWNED JESUS THE CHRIST.

DAVID ANOINTED AS KING

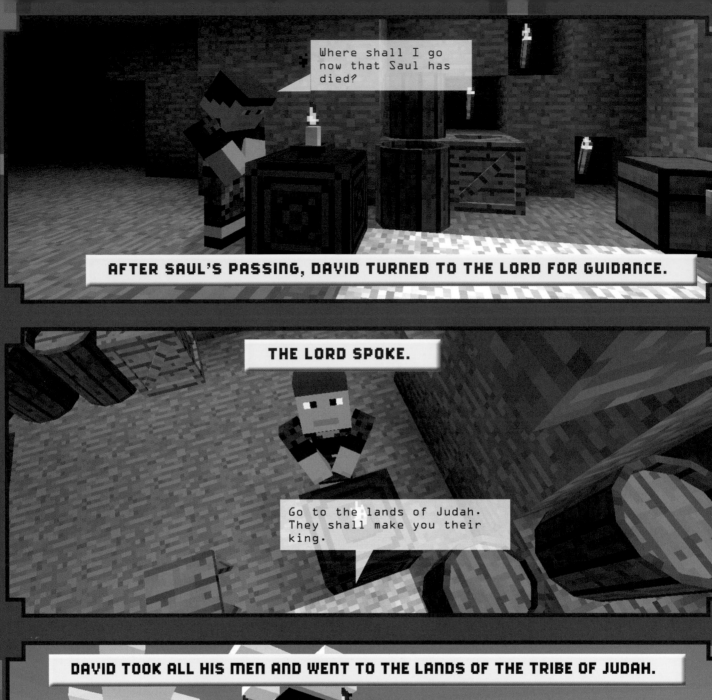

Where shall I go now that Saul has died?

AFTER SAUL'S PASSING, DAVID TURNED TO THE LORD FOR GUIDANCE.

THE LORD SPOKE.

Go to the lands of Judah. They shall make you their king.

DAVID TOOK ALL HIS MEN AND WENT TO THE LANDS OF THE TRIBE OF JUDAH.

David is now king of Judah.

WHEN THE MEN OF JUDAH HEARD THAT DAVID HAD COME, THEY CELEBRATED AND MADE HIM THEIR KING.

General Abner shall lead our military forces.

MEANWHILE, SAUL'S TOP GENERALS NAMED SAUL'S LAST SON, ISH-BO-SHETH, KING OF ISRAEL. IN TURN, ISH-BO-SHETH GAVE GENERAL ABNER COMPLETE CONTROL OF THE MILITARY FORCES.

ABNER MARCHED OUT TO JUDAH TO FACE DAVID.

Let's go, men! Ish-Bo-Sheth, we need to face David before he gets too powerful.

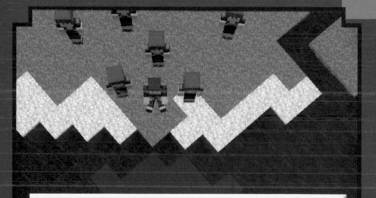

DAVID AND ABNER'S ARMIES MET FACE-TO-FACE.

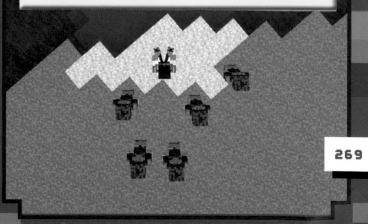

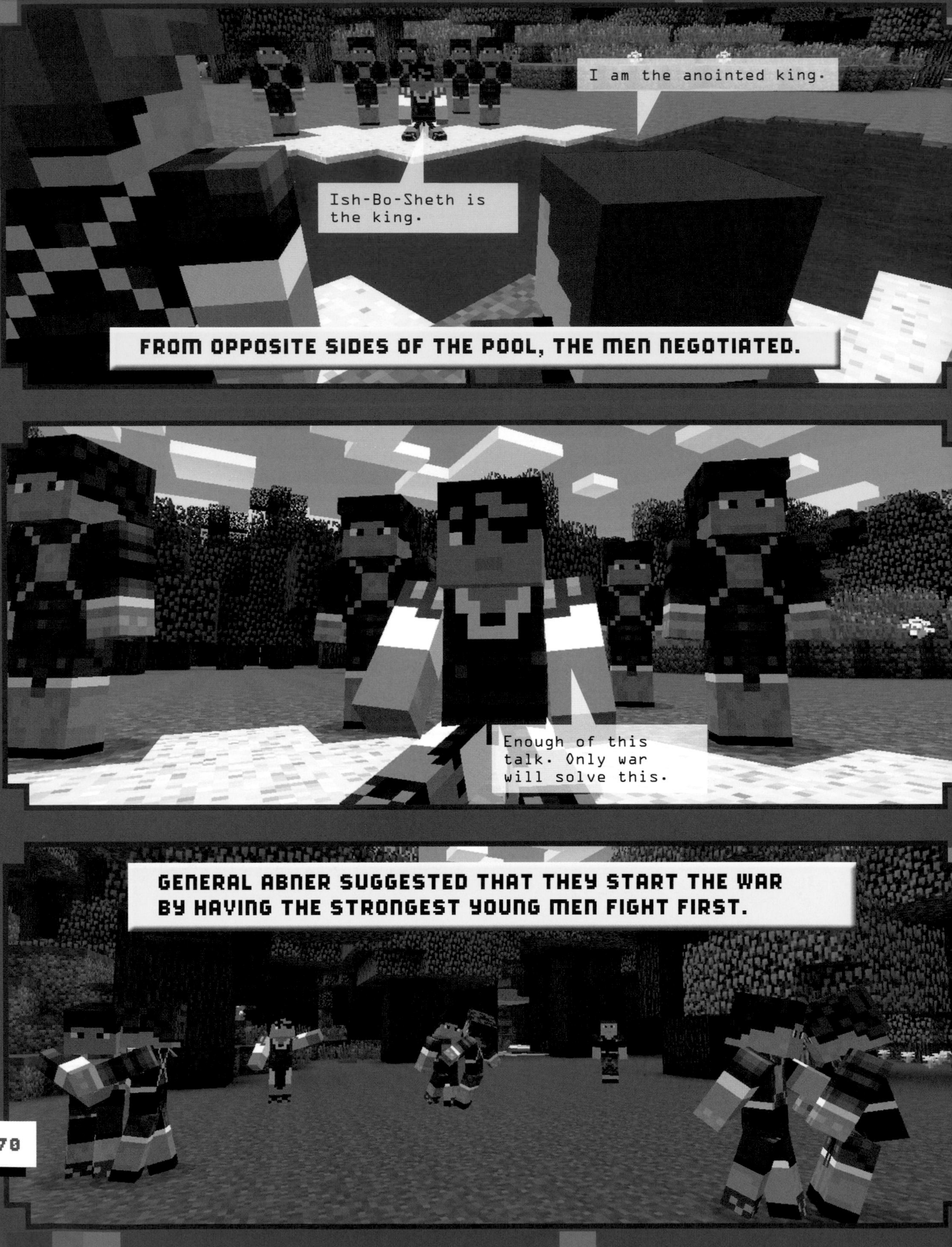
I am the anointed king.
Ish-Bo-Sheth is the king.
FROM OPPOSITE SIDES OF THE POOL, THE MEN NEGOTIATED.
Enough of this talk. Only war will solve this.
GENERAL ABNER SUGGESTED THAT THEY START THE WAR BY HAVING THE STRONGEST YOUNG MEN FIGHT FIRST.

THE WAR BETWEEN THE HOUSE OF SAUL AND THE HOUSE OF DAVID LASTED MANY MOONS.

AS THE WAR WENT ON, DAVID GREW STRONGER AND STRONGER, AND THE HOUSE OF SAUL WEAKER.

FINALLY, ABNER REALIZED THERE WAS LITTLE HOPE FOR HIS ARMY TO WIN. HE HANDED OVER ISRAEL TO DAVID.

AS THE KING, DAVID CHOSE TO MAKE JERUSALEM THE CAPITAL OF THE HEBREW NATION.

You will not take the city.

HOWEVER, THERE WAS A PROBLEM. THE JEBUSITES CONTROLLED JERUSALEM.

NEVERTHELESS, DAVID LED HIS ARMY AND THEY CAPTURED JERUSALEM.

DAVID THEN ORDERED THE ARK TO BE BROUGHT TO JERUSALEM.

AS THE ARK ENTERED INTO THE CITY, THE PEOPLE CHEERED.

DAVID DANCED WITH JOY BEFORE THE LORD.

Panel 1:

God, make me a great king so that I may do Your work and provide Your people with a good life.

THAT NIGHT, DAVID WENT TO THE ROOF OF HIS PALACE AND PRAYED.

Panel 2:

The Lord says: I will make you great.

GOD SPOKE TO THE PROPHET NATHAN AND MADE HIM A PROMISE.

Panel 3:

The Lord will establish a house so great that all will be blessed. I will raise up one who will establish My kingdom for all mankind.

Panel 4:

His is the one who will build a house for me and I will establish the throne of His kingdom forever.

DAVID KNEW THAT GOD WAS TALKING ABOUT A HEAVENLY KINGDOM AND THAT IT WOULD BE HIS HOUSE THAT THE MESSIAH WOULD BE BORN.

274

Is there anyone at the house of Saul that I can show kindness to?

DAVID WAS A MAN WITH A LOVING HEART. HE FELT BAD ABOUT HIS WAR WITH SAUL. HE ASKED HIS SERVANT:

The son of your great friend, Jonathan, still lives. He is poor and crippled. His name is Mephibosheth.

Praise the Lord. Bring the boy here.

DAVID BROUGHT MEPHIBOSHETH INTO HIS HOUSE AND TREATED HIM AS HIS SON.

You shall always be special in God's eyes, and in mine.

ONE NIGHT DAVID WENT TO HIS ROOF AND LOOKED OUT OVER THE CITY.

FROM HIS VANTAGE POINT, HE NOTICED A BEAUTIFUL WOMAN ENJOYING THE BALMY BREEZE OF DUSK.

THE NEXT DAY, DAVID WENT BACK TO THE ROOF AND SENT FOR HIS SERVANT.

Who is the woman that lives next to the palace?

Her name is Bathsheba.

DAVID SENT A MESSAGE TO BATHSHEBA WITH A MARRIAGE PROPOSAL.

DAVID AND BATHSHEBA WERE MARRIED.

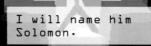
I will name him
Solomon.

THEY HAD A SON, SOLOMON, WHO GREW UP
TO BECOME THE WISEST KING EVER TO LIVE.

SOLOMON

THE TIME CAME WHEN DAVID COULD FEEL HIS LIFE'S END WAS NEAR. HE CALLED BATHSHEBA TO HIS SIDE.

Solomon will be king after me.

My son, Solomon, shall be king when my time passes.

DAVID CALLED NATHAN THE PROPHET AND ZADOK THE PRIEST TO HIS SIDE.

Take Solomon to Gihon. There, have Zadok and Nathan anoint him king in front of all of Israel.

AS THEIR KING INSTRUCTED, ZADOK AND NATHAN ESCORTED SOLOMON THROUGH THE CITY.

THE PEOPLE CHANTED, "LONG LIVE KING SOLOMON!"

ZADOK AND NATHAN TOOK SOLOMON TO GIHON FOR HIS INDUCTION IN FRONT OF THE MASSES.

THE HORNS PLAYED AND ALL REJOICED IN THE NEW KING.

Listen to me, please.

I am here, father.

DAVID THEN CALLED SOLOMON TO HIS SIDE.

Observe what the Lord requires. Walk in obedience to Him. Do this so that our bloodline and our people may prosper.

Goodbye, father.

AFTER SPEAKING TO SOLOMON, DAVID CLOSED HIS EYES FOR THE LAST TIME TO REST WITH HIS ANCESTORS.

THEY BURIED DAVID WITHIN A TOMB IN THE CITY HE FOUNDED FOR ISRAEL.

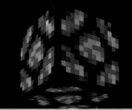

Lord, You have made Your servant king.

SOLOMON FOLLOWED HIS FATHER'S ADVICE AND PRAYED TO GOD.

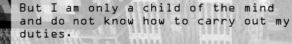

But I am only a child of the mind and do not know how to carry out my duties.

So grant me a discerning heart and great mind with wisdom to lead Your people.

I will grant you what you have asked. Moreover, I will give you even more: You will be given wealth and honor.

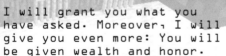

THE LORD WAS PLEASED WITH WHAT SOLOMON ASKED AND SPOKE TO HIM.

283

Do we have all we need?

Yes, all is here.

SOLOMON BEGAN BUILDING THE LORD'S TEMPLE.

THE TEMPLE THAT KING SOLOMON BUILT FOR THE LORD WAS SIXTY CUBITS LONG, TWENTY WIDE.

IT WAS GOING TO BE THIRTY CUBITS HIGH.

THE PORTICO AT THE FRONT WAS TWENTY CUBITS WIDE AND PROJECTS TEN CUBITS OUT.

285

HE MADE NARROW WINDOWS HIGH UP IN THE TEMPLE WALLS. HE BUILT A STRUCTURE AROUND THE BUILDING.

THE LABORERS SOON COMPLETED THE TEMPLE TO SOLOMON'S SPECIFICATIONS, ADDING BEAMS AND CEDAR PLANKS.

KING SOLOMON SUMMONED THE PRIESTS TO BRING FORTH THE ARK. HE WOULD PLACE IT IN THE MAGNIFICENT TEMPLE HE BUILT FOR THE LORD.

THE PRIESTS PAUSED BEFORE THE MIGHTY TEMPLE DOORS SO THAT SOLOMON COULD ADDRESS THE PRIESTS AND ONLOOKERS. ALL WHO WERE PRESENT PRAISED THE LORD WITH SHOUTS TO THE HEAVENS.

SOLOMON SOAKED IN THE MOMENT, WAITING FOR THE CROWD TO QUIET, BEFORE HE GAVE HIS DEDICATION TO THE LORD.

Lord, there is none like You. You who have kept Your covenant of love. You who have kept Your promises.

SOLOMON WALKED TO THE DOORS OF THE TEMPLE AND CONTINUED.

The heavens cannot contain You, much less this temple, but hear our prayers when we pray toward this symbol of our faith in You.

May this symbol of God's presence also commit the hearts of the people to love our Lord, and remain true to His word.

ELIJAH, THE MAN OF MIRACLES

KING SOLOMON RULED WISELY AND JUSTLY UNTIL HIS DEATH.

HE WAS BURIED BESIDE HIS FATHER, DAVID. FOLLOWING SOLOMON, MANY KINGS RULED OVER ISRAEL, BUT MOST OF THEM WERE NOT MEN OF GOD.

EVENTUALLY, KING AHAB CAME TO THE THRONE, AND GOD HAD ENOUGH OF HIS PEOPLE BEING LED ASTRAY.

Elijah, I have chosen you to be my prophet. Go to King Ahab and deliver my message.

AS INSTRUCTED, ELIJAH WENT BEFORE THE KING.

Hear what the Lord says: Because you turned away from Me and to other gods, I will lift My blessing from you.

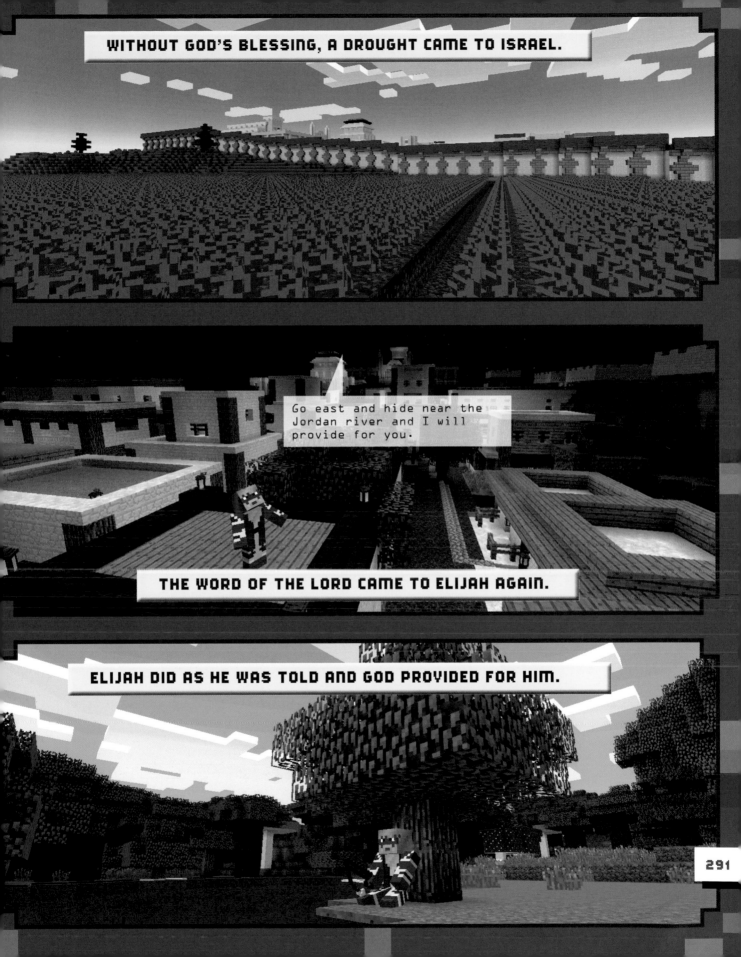

WITHOUT GOD'S BLESSING, A DROUGHT CAME TO ISRAEL.

Go east and hide near the Jordan river and I will provide for you.

THE WORD OF THE LORD CAME TO ELIJAH AGAIN.

ELIJAH DID AS HE WAS TOLD AND GOD PROVIDED FOR HIM.

291

Go to the Zarephath. There, a widow will provide for you.

IN TIME, THE DROUGHT GOT WORSE AND THE RIVER DRIED UP, SO GOD SENT ELIJAH TO MEET A WOMAN WHO COULD HELP HIM.

Greetings, my name is Elijah and God sent me to you.

WHEN ELIJAH REACHED THE CITY, THE WOMAN WAS AT THE GATE.

Would you please bring me some bread? I am hungry.

THE WIDOW THEN EXPLAINED HER SITUATION.

Do not be afraid. Go home and make me a loaf of bread. Then make bread for you and your son. God will provide.

I do not have any bread, only flour in a jar and a little olive oil. It is the last of our food.

For this is what the Lord says: The jar of flour and oil will not be used up until the day it rains.

THE WOMAN WENT HOME AND MADE BREAD THAT DAY AND EVERY DAY AFTER.

The jars, they do not empty!

SOME TIME LATER, THE WIDOW'S SON BECAME ILL AND DIED.

Lord, let this boy live.

ELIJAH CAME TO THE BOY'S ROOM AND CRIED OUT TO THE LORD.

Thank you, loving and merciful Lord!

My son is alive! Praise the living God!

THE LORD HEARD ELIJAH'S CRY AND LIFE RETURNED TO THE BOY.

Go and present yourself to Ahab, king of Israel.

I am afraid he will hurt me, but I will do what You ask of me, Lord, for I have faith.

IN THE THIRD YEAR OF THE DROUGHT, THE WORD OF THE LORD CAME TO ELIJAH.

GOING TO AHAB WAS DANGEROUS FOR ELIJAH, BECAUSE AHAB BLAMED HIM FOR THE DROUGHT.

Why have you come before me? To cause more suffering?

It is not me. Your worship of other gods has brought this suffering on our people.

Now summon the people of Israel to Mount Carmel. Bring your greatest prophets of Baal, and there, I will show you the power of the one true God.

Bring me four hundred and fifty prophets. We will show Elijah that our god is just as good.

SO AHAB SENT WORD THROUGHOUT ALL OF ISRAEL.

AT MOUNT CARMEL, ELIJAH WENT BEFORE THE PEOPLE OF ISRAEL.

People of Israel, how long will you waver between God Almighty and Baal?

I will show you the might of the Lord. Prepare two sacrifices. Then call on your false gods to answer you with fire.

TWO ALTARS WERE PREPARED AND THE SACRIFICES WERE PLACED ON THE ALTARS.

Call on your gods and I will call on the name of the Lord.

FROM MORNING . . .

UNTIL EVENING, THE FALSE PROPHETS CALLED UPON THEIR FALSE GODS THROUGH DANCE AND CHANTS, BUT NO FIRE CAME.

297

Oh Lord, let it be known today that You are God. Answer me so that these people will know that You are God Almighty.

THEN, THE FIRE OF THE LORD FELL ON THE ALTAR AND BURNED UP EVERYTHING.

The Lord is the one true God.

He is God.

The Lord is my God.

Forgive us, Lord!

ELIJAH THEN RAN ALL THE PRIESTS OF BAAL FROM ISRAEL.

WITH THE PEOPLE NOW WORSHIPPING THE ONE TRUE GOD, THE RAIN CAME AND ELIJAH'S WORK WAS DONE. WHEN HIS TIME ON EARTH WAS THROUGH, ELIJAH WAS TAKEN UP TO HEAVEN IN A FIERY CHARIOT.

JONAH AND THE WHALE

Boy, that David is quite a star!

After David will come a series of prophets who continue to illuminate the masses with My message. One in particular, however, is quite stubborn.

Jonah, the time has come for you to journey to another land. The people of Nineveh need some guidance. Pack your things up and go help them.

GOD SENT PROPHETS TO ISRAEL TO SPREAD HIS MESSAGE. ONE SUCH PROPHET WAS JONAH. GOD TOLD HIM TO GO TO A CITY CALLED NINEVEH TO TELL THE PEOPLE TO REPENT FOR THEIR SINFUL WAYS.

THE PEOPLE OF NINEVEH WERE VIOLENT. JONAH WAS SCARED, SO HE SAILED TO ANOTHER CITY INSTEAD.

Where do you want to head?

Anywhere that is far away from Nineveh.

302

HE GOT ON A SHIP THAT WAS HEADED TO NOWHERE IN PARTICULAR.

GOD DREW FORTH THE MIGHTY WINDS TO STIR UP A STORM, PREVENTING THE SHIP FROM GOING ANY FURTHER. THE MEN ON THE SHIP WERE AFRAID.

Jonah, you said you were a prophet to the One True God. Pray to Him so that we may be saved.

THE CAPTAIN OF THE SHIP WENT TO JONAH AND ROUSED HIM FROM HIS SLEEP.

Some of my men say you are to blame for this...

I am afraid that no prayer will help us.

SOME OF THE MEN CONVINCED THE CAPTAIN IT WAS JONAH'S FAULT. JONAH HAD A BAD FEELING THEY WERE RIGHT.

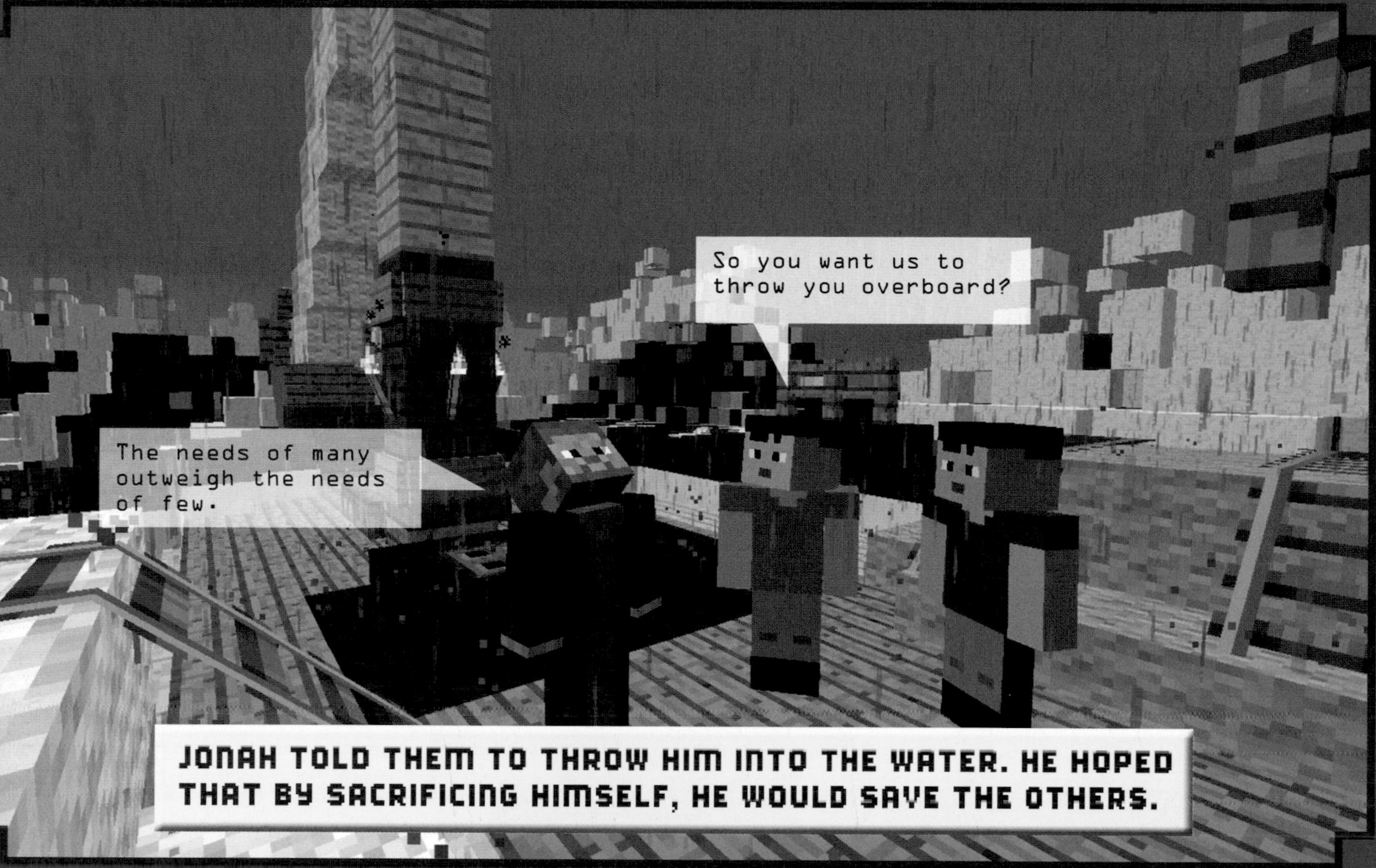
The needs of many
outweigh the needs
of few.
So you want us to
throw you overboard?
JONAH TOLD THEM TO THROW HIM INTO THE WATER. HE HOPED
THAT BY SACRIFICING HIMSELF, HE WOULD SAVE THE OTHERS.

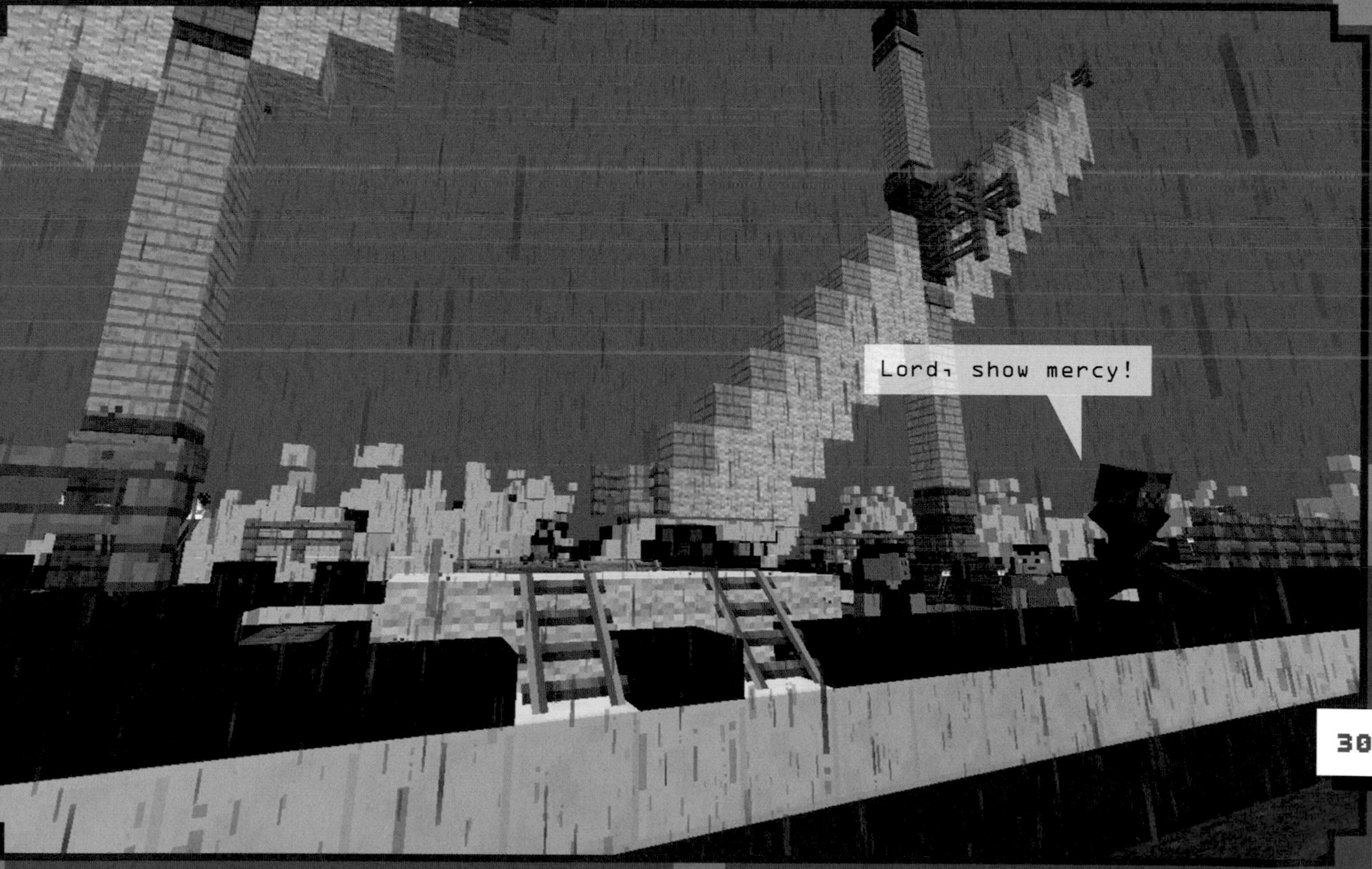
Lord, show mercy!

AS SOON AS JONAH WAS OVERBOARD, THE WATERS BEGAN TO CALM AND THE WAVES GREW LESS INTENSE.

AS THE SHIP MOVED FURTHER AWAY FROM JONAH, A MASSIVE CREATURE EMERGED FROM THE DEEP. WITH ONE BIG GULP, JONAH WAS SWALLOWED UP BY THE WHALE.

JONAH WAS IN THE WHALE FOR THREE DAYS AND THREE NIGHTS. HE PROMISED TO OBEY GOD IF HIS LIFE WAS SPARED.

THE WHALE DID NOT EAT JONAH. IT CARRIED HIM TO DRY LAND AND SPAT HIM OUT. AGAIN, GOD TOLD JONAH TO GO TO NINEVEH.

JONAH OBEYED AND WENT TO NINEVEH. HE GAVE SERMONS AND SPEECHES, TELLING THE PEOPLE TO REPENT OR NINEVEH WOULD BE DESTROYED.

THE PEOPLE REPENTED. THEY FASTED AND PRAYED TO THE ONE TRUE GOD, AND THE LORD SPARED THEM.

DANIEL AND THE LION'S DEN

IN THE THIRD YEAR OF THE REIGN OF JEHOAKIM OF JUDAH, THE KING OF BABYLON CAME AND CONQUERED JERUSALEM.

THE YOUNG MEN OF JERUSALEM WERE TAKEN AS SLAVES.

SOME WERE CHOSEN TO BE THE KING'S SERVANTS, WHILE OTHERS WERE PUT TO HARD LABOR. ONE OF THESE MEN WAS NAMED DANIEL.

IN TIME, THE PEOPLE OF MEDE CONQUERED BABYLON AND A NEW KING SAT ON THE THRONE OF JERUSALEM. DANIEL ENDEARED HIMSELF TO THE NEW KING, DARIUS.

I will put you in charge of the whole kingdom, Daniel.

AT THIS, THE OTHER ADMINISTRATORS BECAME JEALOUS OF DANIEL.

I hate these upstarts.

How is it that we must serve Daniel?

We must find a way to hurt him.

What do you have for me?

THE JEALOUS ADMINISTRATORS WANTED TO CONVINCE THE KING TO MAKE A NEW LAW.

The people should pray to you for the next thirty days.

If they break the law, they'll be thrown into the lions' den.

I have an idea! Let's go to the king.

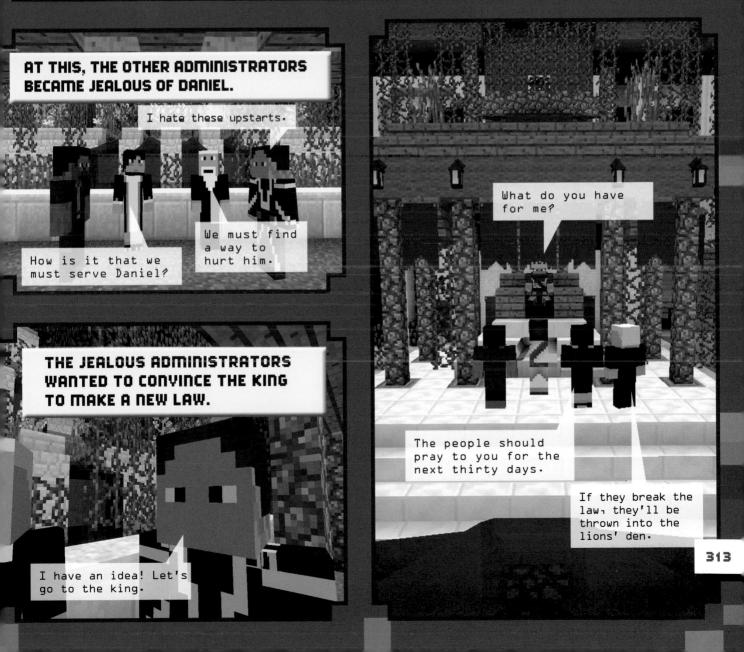

313

I have to worship King Darius? This is wrong in God's eyes.

The people shall worship Darius for the next 30 days.

For law breakers will be thrown into the lion's den.

SO KING DARIUS PUT THE DECREE IN WRITING FOR ALL TO SEE.

We'll follow him, and when Daniel prays to his God, we will get him.

WHEN DANIEL LEARNED OF THE LAW, HE WENT HOME AND PRAYED TO GOD TO PROTECT HIM.

I knew this would work.

I'll get dibs on his house when he is gone.

Now we have him.

IMMEDIATELY, THE ADMINISTRATORS WENT TO KING DARIUS.

We have found a lawbreaker, my lord.

Tell me who.

No, not my beloved servant!

It is Daniel!

315

DARIUS CALLED DANIEL TO HIM.

I am guilty only of loving the one true God.

Please, Daniel, say it is not so?

There must be some way.

DARIUS THOUGHT ABOUT HIS PREDICAMENT AND WHAT HE COULD DO TO SAVE DANIEL.

It is time.

THE ADMINISTRATORS CAME AT SUNRISE TO DARIUS FOR HIS VERDICT.

WITH THE PRESSURE OF THE LEADERS, THE KING GAVE THE ORDER AND HAD DANIEL ARRESTED.

I am sorry, Daniel. May your God protect you.

I will pray to God.

My God will be with me.

I am a fool and now an innocent man must suffer.

May your God you serve rescue you.

THEY LOWERED DANIEL DOWN AND PREPARED TO SEAL THE DEN.

318 DANIEL PRAYED TO THE LORD FOR HIS SALVATION. THE LORD SENT AN ANGEL, WHO CLOSED THE MOUTHS OF THE LIONS.

THAT NIGHT, THE KING DID NOT EAT NOR HAVE ANY ENTERTAINMENT. HE COULD NOT SLEEP AND PACED THE PARAPETS OF HIS PALACE.

AT FIRST LIGHT, THE KING HURRIED TO THE LIONS' DEN, CALLING OUT TO DANIEL.

Daniel, servant of the living God. Are you still alive?

My God sent His angel to shut the mouths of the lions.

319

Your God is truly
the living Lord.
Praise Him above
all others.

DANIEL WAS TAKEN FROM THE DEN AND RESTORED TO HIS POSITION IN THE KINGDOM.

A DECREE WENT OUT THROUGHOUT THE LAND.

All who live in the
kingdom of Israel must
worship the God of
Daniel.

ACKNOWLEDGMENTS

TO OUR READERS:

First of all, thank you for taking time to pick up this book. We hope that you've enjoyed reading it as much as we did making it. As middle school teachers, we have always maintained a passion for projects where we could experiment with new curriculum and teaching practices through technology. When we started the Advanced Learning Project years ago, we had no idea it would lead us down so many varied paths, starting with summer camps in robotics, rocketry, and computer building, which evolved into developing Craft-Academy, our Minecraft education platform and curriculum. We host educational Minecraft servers, and write books that take place in Minecraft worlds. We feel truly blessed that we have been given the opportunity to share our creative educational endeavors with the world.

Putting a project like this together requires a team effort, and for that, we would like to acknowledge a few people:

We wouldn't be making these books if it were not for our editor Krishan Trotman. She found us, she believed in us, and we thank her deeply for the opportunity.

Big thanks to Noppes for the support he provided us using his Custom NPCs and More Player Models 2 mods.

Thanks to our assistant developer George Higashiyama, and, of course, our students—you know who you are!

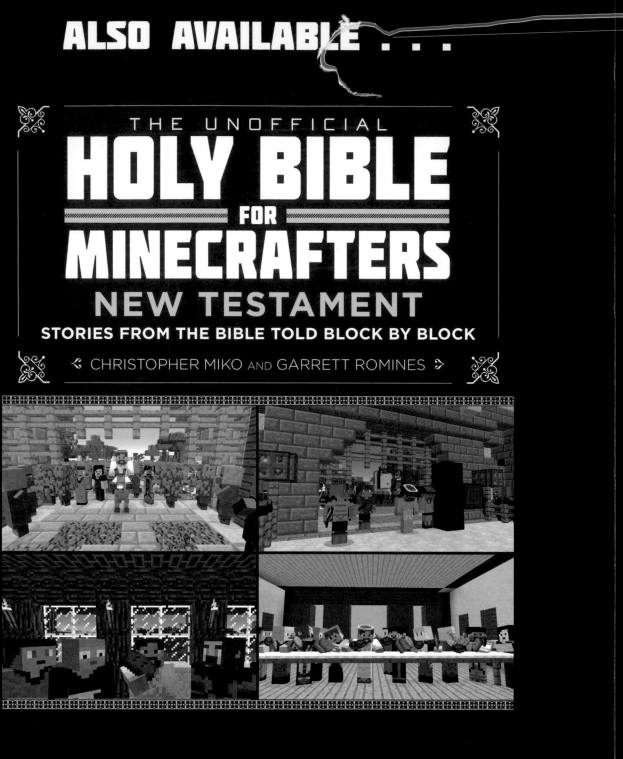